What's a
# Smart
# woman
*like you* doing
# At
# Home?
Revised edition

# What's a Smart woman *like you* doing At Home?

Revised edition

Linda Burton
Janet Dittmer
Cheri Loveless

Published by
Mothers at Home™

# To our husbands

Published by

**Mothers At Home**™

8310-A Old Courthouse Road

Vienna, Virginia 22182

**Mothers At Home**™ is a nonprofit 501(C)3 organization devoted to the support of mothers who choose (or would like to choose) to stay at home to nurture their families. In addition to this and other materials, Mothers At Home™ also publishes Welcome Home®, a monthly journal that puts mothers at home across the country in touch with each other. For information on **Welcome Home**® and other **Mothers At Home**™ publications, please write to:

Mothers At Home
8310-A Old Courthouse Road
Vienna, Virginia 22182

**Library of Congress Cataloging-in-Publication Data**

Burton, Linda, 1946-

What's a smart woman like you doing at home?/Linda Burton, Janet Dittmer, Cheri Loveless. — Rev. ed.

1. Housewives—United States.

2. Mothers—United States.

3. Housewives—United States—Psychology.

I. Dittmer, Janet, 1948- . II. Loveless, Cheri, 1951- . III. Title.

HQ759.B785  1992   306.8′743—dc20   92-22259

ISBN 0-9631188-1-1

# Acknowledgments

Everyone who has children knows that mothers — especially mothers of young children — don't have time to write books. That is why this part of the book is so important.

The first round of thanks goes to our husbands, without whom this book would not exist. The hours they have invested in encouraging us, comforting us, and inspiring us cannot be measured, although they may be tempted to count the number of diapers changed, dishes washed, errands run....

The next curtain call is for our children — thirteen of them among us, ranging in age from one to eleven years old. They have, on most days at least, remained patient with disrupted household routines (except in Cheri's house where there is no routine), suffered without complaint through more television than we would recommend (except in Janet's house where there is no television), and consumed an inordinate amount of fudgesicles (especially Linda's kids, who have always had too many because of a vow she made when she was denied one once at the age of eight).

Next in line are:

• The many family members, friends, and neighbors who invited our children over to play on those days we had to have a few hours of quiet, and who surprised us with meals and treats and notes of encouragement when we least expected it and most needed it. A special thanks goes to Cheri's sister, Tina, and Linda's mother, Helen; another goes to Lynne, who pitched in cheerfully with all six of Cheri's children when the book deadline was extended past the closing day of school.

• The volunteers and staff of **Mothers At Home** and *Welcome Home*, who have helped us with everything from analyzing and philosophizing to xeroxing and reading rough drafts. We are especially grateful to Heidi Brennan, Holly Coyne, and Kathryn Della-Piana on the Mothers At Home Board of Directors, who took over many of our duties within the organization so we would have time to write a book in the first place, and to our office manager, Phyllis Bryson, and her assistant, Julie Burnett, who helped us with the preliminary selection of letters. We also appreciate the diligent effort and generous time given by Cindy Richetti in copyediting the manuscript.

• The thousands of women who have written to us, who expressed their feelings so beautifully and with such candor that we could not help but respond to their need to be heard. We are particularly grateful to those women who gave us permission to quote them in the text of this book. We have tried to honor the manner in which they requested to be identified.

• Howard Hayghe at the U.S. Bureau of Labor Statistics who kindly answered our detailed questions while toddlers freely explored his office, and who made further explanations by telephone whenever we would request them.

• Christine Davidson, author of *Staying Home Instead*, and Deborah Fallows, author of *A Mother's Work*, for sharing information and for challenging social taboos on the subject of staying at home.

And finally, we want to thank each other. Certainly this is one book that would not have been written without the extraordinary efforts of every member of the team. While we have all contributed major ideas, entire paragraphs of text, and final judgment calls (both philosophical and editorial), we want to acknowledge the unique roles each of us played:

Linda wrote all but a few of the personal essays included here. We considered (over her strong objections) publishing her essays and forgetting the rest of the book. She also sparked many of the ideas for Part II, rejuvenated numerous tired sentences throughout the basic text, and served as our walking thesaurus whenever we needed just the right word (and sometimes when we didn't). Her theatrics as she recounted the trials of her life as a mother kept us laughing throughout the project, including during the darker hours when we were sure we could never produce a manuscript at all.

Janet coordinated the selection of letters from among literally thousands of possibilities. We stood in awe of her ability to organize, categorize, and cross-reference so thoroughly that the perfect quote was never further away than her famous "master" file. We also relied heavily on her knowledgeable and sensitive editorial judgment. Though she continually insisted that she is not a writer, she provided the first drafts for most of the chapters in Part II, contributed two essays, and deserves credit for the "completion" of four of the proposed twelve chapters of the book by cleverly organizing us out of the need for them. We still marvel at the thought that anyone would read *The Chicago Manual of Style* for fun or that someone who actually has the self-discipline to exercise every weekday could feel guilty occasionally indulging her passion for chocolate.

Cheri, who served as the informal, ever tranquil overseer and manager of the project, was able to pull together the final text of a whole book from a few words and a lot of feelings. She pointed the way around impasses and out of jams, while nursing a baby, ministering to poison ivy, and monitoring the daily progress of four science fair projects. While everyone else was suggesting abandoning the book in favor of trips to the Bahamas, it was Cheri who never stopped working, and never stopped caring.

Finally, thank *you* for deciding to look at this book. We hope you will benefit from the journey into motherhood that will come with reading it.

*    *    *

Since our book was first published in 1986 (Acropolis Books), countless mothers have committed their time and talents to carry on the work of **Mothers At Home**. We are indebted to the Board of Directors, Management Team, staff, and volunteers, whose hard work has made it possible to revise and republish this book.

We offer special thanks to Heidi Brennan and Catherine Myers for helping us revise Chapter Seven; to Heidi for researching current statistics, helping to revise Chapter Six, and handling the contract agreements; and to Catherine for managing the overall publication. We appreciate the dedicated work of Janet Palmisano for coordinating many of the production steps; and of Tammy DeMartino and Alice Lee who contributed significantly to the publication process. Mary Ellen McCormick has developed and analyzed *Welcome Home* readership studies, which have been a great help to us and for which we are very appreciative. We also thank those who helped to keyboard the text: Alice Lee, Cheryl Fischer Breckinridge, Lilli Hausenfluck, Katrina Sweitzer, and Kathy Thomas. We are grateful for the proofreading and thoughtful editing suggestions of Laura Jones (proofreading coordinator), Cheryl Fischer Breckinridge, Lilli Hausenfluck, and Betsy Kocsis. We also thank Kathleen Richman who typeset the book and helped significantly with its new format.

# Contents

# Choosing Success
# at Home

**W**e have written this book for the many, many mothers who share the feelings and convictions in these pages — who until recently may never have seen them expressed in print. We think these women deserve to know that in spite of appearances to the contrary, women who are rediscovering the merits of home and the pleasures of rearing children are not alone. In fact, they are a majority.

Our purpose is not to promote a philosophy, but to share a discovery. In 1983, when we began publishing a newsletter for mothers who choose to stay home, we had not yet reached many of the conclusions outlined here. We knew then that there were other mothers like us: women who had consciously chosen to devote their good minds and considerable skills to rearing their children. We also knew that these women frequently felt isolated and frustrated by inaccurate but popularized stereotypes. By creating a national newsletter where mothers at home could speak to each other, we hoped to reach out to them.

When our publication, *Welcome Home*, made its debut, the press took an interest in our contention that more and more women were choosing to stay home over other attractive options. One newspaper article led to another and to radio interviews and television appearances. In response, we received a torrent of letters from across the country. Within weeks of our first press interview, they numbered in the thousands.

These letters told a story whose breadth and depth even we did not suspect. We heard from rural mothers and urban mothers, conservatives and liberals, those with money and those just scraping by — from mothers who had always stayed home and mothers who were still working full-time. Yet, in spite of such contrasts in background, each letter seemed to have the same underlying message: Rearing my children is much more challenging and fulfilling than I was led to believe. In spite of the current pressure to work full-time, and at the expense of previous personal goals, I want to spend these years at home with my children.

We began to realize we were witnessing a revolution of sorts. Thousands, possibly millions, of women were purposefully choosing to abandon long-accepted assumptions about their own lives in order to do something they thought no other women were doing. Each mother — thinking herself one of an unappreciated few — was altering carefully crafted plans for her own future because she had learned firsthand that being at home as much as possible directly influenced the quality of life for both herself and her family.

However, what we were hearing from all these mothers in all fifty states and abroad differed greatly from what we were reading in most newspapers and magazines. Chic career women with "power" wardrobes and Elysian lifestyles dominated both the articles and the ads. Nationally read publications, from *Women's Day* to *Parents* to *The Washington Post* regularly heralded the arrival of ever-increasing numbers of mothers in the work force every year. Mothers at home, if mentioned at all, were set apart as a quaint and rapidly vanishing breed.

Interestingly, such conclusions seemed to be based on three sources: the U.S. Department of Labor (DOL) statistics, several oft-quoted childcare studies, and interviews with a handful of mothers. When we reviewed the same sources, we found that the DOL statistics, when understood in context, tell quite a different story; that many studies are rife with "exceptions" that in fact make up the rule; and that mothers who work and mothers who stay home have much more in common than they have to argue about.

*What's a Smart Woman Like You Doing at Home?* reveals what today's mothers are really feeling. In both essay and explanation, with quotes from many of our candid and unsolicited letters, this book exposes the gap between what the media says about mothers and what mothers say about themselves.

America's mothers have spoken. In this book, we tell you what they have told us.

> *Linda Burton*
> *Janet Dittmer*
> *Cheri Loveless*

# Part One

# Searching for Supermom & Discovering Home

*Chapter One*

# A New Mother Emerges

**A** few years ago in a women's studies course at a college in upstate New York, a bright, young coed from Washington, D.C. began to feel uneasy about what she was hearing in class. An ambitious girl, with clear-cut career goals, she nevertheless found herself offended at the way the professor completely ignored the issue of traditional family life. Although she had no immediate plans to begin a family, she knew women who did; and she had great respect for the significant contribution her mother had made by staying home to rear three daughters. She observed that questions were posed in such a way as to make any student who might want to explore alternatives to a full-time career feel ridiculous. Yet, subsequent discussions with classmates and friends revealed that many of them — even those who felt strongly about pursuing a career — still hoped eventually to meet someone, settle down, and have a family. One day a question about the choice to be at home was finally raised in class, to which the professor responded, "That wouldn't apply to anyone here. Women today want to do something more important with their lives."

Thus a college professor joined many others in dismissing what they all believe to be an unenlightened and dwindling population of women.

They are wrong.

Women who are rearing their own children at home today are neither unenlightened nor dwindling. As a group, they are increasing in numbers; and as individuals, they are keenly aware of both their opportunities and their potential.

## Women at Home Today Are There by Choice

A whole new generation of mothers rocks the cradle today. They are savvy to their rights and aware of their choices. And though they have been raised with the notion that a woman's greatest contribution lies outside the home, they are discovering — sometimes to their great surprise — that they want to devote more time to tending the hearth and caring for their children. At a time when women can choose among an array of exciting possibilities, more and more mothers are deciding to stay home and invest their energies in a very tangible future — the next generation.

In fact, it is difficult today to find a woman who is unhappily "stuck" at home. Rather, most women who stay home are there because of enormous conviction about the importance of what they do. Bonnie Albus, a mother of two teens, in Kailua, Hawaii, reflects the feelings of many: "I chose to stay at home after the birth of our first child. I chose this career in the same thoughtful way people choose to be nurses, dentists, doctors, singers, artists, engineers, or teachers. It's a career which I find more demanding, more joy filled, more time consuming, and more thrilling than any other career I have been engaged in." She adds, "How many people can truly say that their 'job' is a passionate commitment which is deeply satisfying? Certainly any

---

*I'm a registered nurse (retired) and between graduation and first child worked ten years. Once I had my son, who is now twenty-seven, I became a full-time mother, as I felt nothing else was more important and I never regretted it. At age forty-one, I had a daughter; this was before it was the fashion to have children at a later age, and I received a lot of strange looks. (In between, I had four miscarriages.) Today, as I look out the window in the morning, and watch the wives and mothers shivering in the cold, scraping ice and snow off their cars, while I can go back for another cup of coffee and a leisurely reading of the paper, I wonder which of us is more liberated.*

*It seems to me the main problem with women's groups, for either side, is their narrow point of view — it is their way or it is wrong. How dare they try to tell anyone else what choice to make! It's an individual decision as to what's best for that particular woman and her family. Too often, the family is forgotten, and "what's best for me" is all that's considered, and sometimes it has disastrous effects. It's true, some women have no choice because of financial reasons, but they're not the ones I'm talking about. I realize my generation was raised differently, but I, personally, had a choice, and who was more qualified than I to make it? I really enjoyed working, at the time, and for eight hours a day I was "important"; but at home, for twenty-four hours a day, I am loved.*

*Florabel Davis, R.N., Randallstown, Maryland*

---

A New Mother Emerges

group of people who could make that claim would include a great many mothers who have chosen to stay at home."

For some, this choice drastically alters earlier visions of working outside the home throughout motherhood. For others, it represents a promise to their children that was made before the first child was even conceived. But whether a woman always planned on being home full-time or whether at first she assumed she would continue in the workplace, her choice is usually a deliberate one. In today's world, women stay home because they want to stay home.

Contrary to popular belief, this desire to be available full-time to one's children is not limited to women who have preconceived ideas about "a woman's place," nor is it merely an excuse offered by tired supermoms who lack the ability to "do it all." Though personal philosophy and past experience remain a major influence on a woman's choice, the actual commitment to stay home is rarely based on precon-ditioned attitudes or logic alone. Mothers decide to stay home not just because they are tired of juggling family and career; not just because they want to "be there" for the first word and the first step; not just because they have found that a rich home life requires persistent personal investment. They want to be home because in some quiet moment caring for their children, they have suddenly experienced the vastness, the intricacies, the delicate nature of this work. While per-forming some entirely routine act of nurturing, they have unexpect-edly stumbled on a moment of insight so luminous as to reveal with imposing clarity that the greatest opportunity for success they might ever have is nestled right there in their arms. And in the midst of a thousand previous assumptions about life and love, in an instant that

---

*It was a difficult decision to make — relinquishing my chosen career to go into a completely unrelated field. I had invested ten challenging, exciting, and joyful years in my sales career. It was only after six months of careful deliberation that I decided to trade sales presentations, meetings, travel, and the confidence that comes from experience for this new uncharted territory — the diapering, feeding and full-time nurturing of my first child.*

*I hadn't realized, until I no longer had my sales position, how much I was defined by my career. How would I incorporate this new label, "homemaker," into my personality? The respect I desire from others for my decision to stay home has to first come from within myself. If I am apologetic about my new role, I won't have, and can't expect, respect from others. But if I am satisfied with myself and filled with self-respect, I will project that image to my family and friends.*

*Lynn Viale, Gilroy, California*

---

no one else can measure or see, they decide that this uncertain business of trying to guide childish innocence into adult wisdom is an art worthy of extraordinary exertion and time.

## Choosing Home — An Unrecognized Trend

The growing desire to solidly devote a season of life to the nurturing of others, and to do it by spending as much time as possible at home, is not a passing fad. Neither is it a bandwagon to jump aboard in the wake of a jarring national event nor the activist result of a consciousness-raising book. There is no recognized "movement," no leader, no charismatic public figure exhorting women to stay home. Yet, across the nation, in the isolation of their own homes, unaware of the fact that others are doing likewise, millions of women are arriving at the same conclusion. Knowing they could be successful almost anywhere, they are choosing success at home.

Although the decision to stay home is an intensely personal one, the fact that it is being made by so many women independently clearly suggests a trend: we are seeing the emergence of a brand new kind of mother — a mother with the confidence and emancipation espoused by the feminist movement who also wants to give her children the kind of time and devotion associated with traditional homemaking; a mother who is intent upon putting her family first without putting herself last.

This new mother may well feel uncomfortable with the labels "housewife" and "working mother," because she does not see herself as either one. When she is home, she is doing an awful lot more than

---

*I enjoyed a career in personnel management following graduation from the University of Washington. When our son was born one year ago, the decision was so easy — both my husband and I wanted me to stay home. I don't feel I've given anything up, but rather, I have been given an opportunity to experience a joy I could never have imagined.*

*Beverly Hawley, Edmonds, Washington*

*I believe there is a whole new breed of well-educated, active women who have simply changed careers. The high energy level, intelligence, organizational skills, etc., needed in our past careers have simply been transferred to our new careers as homemakers. All the energy put into our new careers comes directly back in so many wonderfully rewarding ways. Personally, I love my career change to mother and homemaker.*

*Connie Cecys, Arden Hills, Minnesota*

---

keeping house, and if she works she is likely to be working out of a back bedroom or to be working only part-time. In fact, in an effort to keep her original career goals somewhat intact while putting them on hold to rear her children, she often experiments with full-time work, part-time work, volunteer work — sometimes overcommitting her time, then drawing back, then reaching out again — until she finds the right balance of attentiveness to home life and pursuit of outside accomplishments.

At a time when a one-income family cannot always rely on a comfortable lifestyle, these new mothers are willing to make whatever creative arrangements it takes to practice their new priorities. They are learning that leaving the traditional job market does not preclude using and improving income-producing skills — or for that matter, developing new ones. They are discovering that selecting one path over another — no matter how difficult the choice — does not necessarily close doors; rather it forces one to seek out new ways to do old things. So these mothers who want to stay home are shifting to flex-time, dropping to part-time, leaving their jobs to start home businesses — doing whatever it takes to "work it out" so they can pay the bills while reserving as much time as possible for their families.

## Between Schlafly and Steinem—
## Today's Mothers Break New Ground

This new mother is part of a larger group of women who are learning to blend the two crusading, and supposedly conflicting, philosophies which have courted them for decades now. While one philosophy insisted that women become more than mere extensions of the people they serve, the other issued reminders of the joys of nourishing family relationships. While the first encouraged women to gain financial security in the job market and to seek success in places they may not have thought to look a generation ago, the other cautioned against denying certain uniquely feminine qualities and

---

*I am a twenty-four-year-old single girl who could never thank my mother enough for staying home and raising both me and my brother. I someday hope to be able to do the same for children of my own, but believe it or not, most young men of today feel this is absurd. I am very successful in my job and I do enjoy working, but I feel nothing is as important as setting young life on the right path.*
*Gina M. Chalfant, Pittsburgh, Pennsylvania*

---

warned against replacing a less tangible emotional reward with a less desirable material one.

Over the years, these voices have grown angrier and more extreme — and women have grown more confused. They weren't ready to view men as a major public enemy, but they also had no desire to employ insipid feminine wiles to get their way with the sex that held the cards. For most women, burning bras at a public rally or dressing in Saran Wrap to greet their men at the end of the day held equally little appeal.

Now, a new population of women is arising which understands that no one is under any obligation to select between these two ideologies. And in its midst are many, many mothers who are turning a deaf ear to two groups which, for many long years, have simultaneously fought for their allegiance and ignored their needs. Mothers today have listened to the people who claim to speak for them and are now discarding the outrageous in favor of the sensible to forge a philosophy all their own.

From Houston, Texas, Diane Dunham Massey writes: "I am an attorney who became de-liberated by my daughter who is now fourteen months old. Gloria Steinem can no longer be my role model. As I was a pathbreaker ten years ago in the professional arena, I now find myself again a pathbreaker as a professional who chooses to shelve a career, temporarily, to commit myself to raising a family in the best manner possible."

Diane is one of millions of women who find no contradiction in believing they should seek their own identity and financial independence, without necessarily spending large quantities of time away from their children. Until recently, mothers who found themselves espousing this mixture of beliefs thought they were alone. It is

---

*It was wonderful to hear that there are others who feel as I do! I know that the most important job I will ever have is being a good mother to [my children]. The temptation to go back to work is there from time to time. Certainly my working would make things easier for us financially. I have a B.S. degree in secondary education and taught school for six years before "retiring" to the life of a homemaker/mother. Teaching is easier than mothering! But, I know in my heart that I am needed by my children. No one can love them and care for them like I can. I will be able to look back on these years with no regrets. It's nice to know I'm not alone.*

*Linda Perez, Kenner, Louisiana*

A New Mother Emerges

beginning to dawn on them, however, that they aren't the only women in the middle — that maybe even a majority of women are in the middle.

Maureen Allen of Annapolis, Maryland, comments: "I [believe there] to be a growing trend — that is, more and more young mothers are choosing to remain at home with their children to carry out rewarding, stimulating, and self-fulfilling work — raising their children. One doesn't always find these qualities in her 'career' position!"

◆   ◆   ◆

This vibrant mother of the nineties — who understands her options and has confidence in her abilities, who rejects the extreme philosophies she has heard in favor of what really works in her life, who is deciding that additional time with her family is worth more than time spent somewhere else — wants to be home. Yet, abandoning closely held convictions to make way for new revelations is never easy. And so, today's mother, once she gives birth physically, must also struggle with an emotional birth — as she slowly comes to terms with the new realities in her life.

*Chapter Two*

# Heirs to a Movement

**M**otherhood may well be the most controversial profession a woman can enter today. Remarkably, a choice that once seemed natural, even inevitable, now invites open criticism. Whether a woman begins her family early or starts at age thirty-five, carefully plans one child or produces a brood, enrolls her three-year-old in an academic preschool or shuns public education to teach her children at home, she winds up in a pillory facing someone who is willing to throw a tomato. And when it comes to the volatile issue of working full-time versus staying home, the outward criticism is compounded by an unexpected inner turmoil.

## Today's Mothers — 
## Raised with One Philosophy but Taught Another

Most of us now in the midst of our parenting years straddle two incongruous eras of motherhood history. Our own mothers were generally home when we were children; they greeted us after school, drove us to piano lessons, and nagged us to clean our bedroom before going out to play. They were there when we needed to chat, there when we needed advice, there when we needed to cry. Whether positive or negative, we felt the impact their presence had on our lives.

But we were educated in "enlightened" times. While Donna Reed raised her television family in America's living rooms in the afternoon, the emerging leaders of "women's lib" dominated the news shows in the evening. In the hubbub of ideas then competing for society's center stage, a new theme song intensified against the background din, and its strident, egalitarian spirit was both arresting and appealing.

Whatever our reaction to the women's movement's more radical and hotly debated issues, like abortion and gay rights, we saw little reason to argue with its major theme: equal opportunity in the workplace. We believed women should be able to pursue whatever kind of career they wanted. In fact, many of us were eager to try some traditionally male vocations — and confident we would be worth the equal pay.

By the time we headed for college or set out to "make it on our own," a simple but trenchant message spoke from the pages of virtually every book, newspaper, and magazine: "Smart women go to work." Indeed, it seemed treasonous not to, especially in the presence of those who had fought the battles before us, ostensibly on our behalf. Instinctively, we began to search for careers. While some of us had the determination and interest to begin our families in spite of the swelling tide, many of us postponed marriage, or at least having children.

## Hard Questions — Uncertain Answers

However, the day finally came when we wanted children, and could no longer ignore some inevitable maternal issues. In some ways we feared giving up the chance to offer our children the kind of traditional home life we had once enjoyed, but no more than we feared giving up our potential for progress in a demanding yet often satisfying workplace.

Accordingly, we began to ask questions of ourselves. Would our children suffer if we continued to work outside the home? Would our careers suffer if we took several years off to raise a family? It was a rare woman who thought to ask the more pertinent question: "Will I suffer if I try to be true to both worlds?"

Relatively few of us ever felt we had unimpeachable answers to those questions. Nonetheless, we made our choices and went our separate ways. Some of us went home to give our children a sem-

---

*I am a career woman with school-age children, but I sincerely sympathize not only with the working mother at her job away from home, but the working mother at home. Most importantly, it's the children who matter and who suffer for our inadequacies, be it personal or beyond our control.*

*Anne Jaramillo, Barstow, California*

blance of the security we had known in our own homes. Some of us brought our work home or dropped to part-time hours. Still others set out to combine full-time work with full-time family responsibilities — whether to preserve a place on the career ladder, to enhance a particular lifestyle, or simply to put food on the table.

"Supermoms" with dynamic careers and fulfilling family lives began to parade before us in the media spotlight while the rest of us found ourselves stumbling around in the dark. This happy, self-confident, supremely organized woman appeared to glide effortlessly in and out of the intricate corridors of her fascinating life. We looked at her with admiration, but also with a vague hope that maybe she had bad days no one was telling us about. We were bothered that in our lives, reality didn't seem to match her breezy style — in fact, it didn't even come close.

Those of us at home began to wonder if any other mother in the world was still reading to toddlers and carpooling Cub Scouts in the middle of the day. Those of us at work searched in vain for the promised "quality time" with our children, and for ways to avoid shortchanging our husbands, our employers, and ourselves.

The internal interrogation continued, and our questions grew more specific. Was consistent "quality" child care only a mirage that would always disappear the moment it seemed to be within our reach? Would life at home leave us stranded without skills in the event of a tragedy or in our later years? Would we ever see employers sympa-

---

*I am a thirty-three-year-old mother of two, ages three-and-a-half and seven, who needs to know that there are other "mothers at home." I hold a college degree in education and I consider myself to be fairly intelligent. Why is it a curse to be an educated woman (or uneducated) who chooses to stay at home and be a full-time mother?!*

*I believe that women should have the choice: to be mothers or not, to be working mothers or not. Why must women attack each other in defense of their particular lifestyle? Let's all remember that women of our generation (i.e., twenty-five to thirty-five years) have no role models to follow. We are all breaking new ground. It's tough!! We need to respect all the aspects of the newly emerged women's movement. We need to respect the different directions that women take these days.*

*We women boast that we are both intelligent and flexible by nature. Let's start proving it!*

*Carol Neider, East Meadow, New York*

thetic to the plight of a sick child or amenable to the possibility of part-time hours without reduced benefits?

So completely were we surrounded by infallible models of the modern woman that it never occurred to us that we weren't the only ones having a hard time making it all work. For a long time we were sure that if we would just try a little harder or get a little better organized, we would find some magic key that would unlock all the secrets to really, truly "having it all." Finally we began to realize that life was going by a little too fast, and the answers were nowhere in sight. Some of us even began to wonder if the grass was any greener on the other side of the work/home fence, and so we would wander in and out of the work force — quitting work to stay home one year, heading back to a job the next, perhaps only to come home again.

Still, no matter what we decided to do, no matter how good we initially felt about doing it, someone always showed up to tell us we were absolutely, unequivocally wrong.

Motherhood had become synonymous with "guilt."

## We Feel Guilty No Matter What We Choose

Although the superwoman myth has finally begun to fade, our internal battles are far from over. "I have wrestled for the better part of a year with the question of whether or not I should quit my job," Antoinette Cennamo wrote to us. "I am a teacher of English who took two extended child-rearing leaves to care for my sons. Now that they are six and three and I am working full-time, I find myself very unhappy with the quality of our family life."

Living in Levittown, New York, near New York City, Antoinette found that the mothers at home she met in local mothers groups were generally well-to-do and tended to "criticize working mothers for wanting a lifestyle which they themselves enjoy only because they

---

*My wife and I believe strongly that school-age children need Mother at home when they arrive, or are sick, or for numerous other reasons. Perhaps your thrust needs to include the principle that a father's first profession is "father." Any man who recognizes that family comes before job can understand that he is a father first and [his occupation] next. If he's really a father first, he ought to have less trouble viewing and supporting his wife as a mother first. And, at least until the children are through high school, a 100% mother. Other "professional" occupations are subordinate, just as they are to him.*

Arthur B. Cyphers, Naperville, Illinois

---

'married well.'" Her working friends, however, found it hard to understand her desire to quit work to spend more time at home: "My friends think that I have lost my mind. Quitting my job means losing tenure, seniority, a good salary, and a work year that women in business envy as a practically part-time one. The truth is that with travel time I am gone from home eight hours a day, that I am too tired when I come home to provide 'quality time,' and that I am discovering that as children grow older they require different, not less, supervision."

Antoinette did quit work, but only after she unsuccessfully lobbied for a part-time position at more than one school. She now states with confidence: "I have never regretted my decision. While a salary can be earned again and professional recognition and tenure achieved again, the precious years with my boys could never, ever be regained." Still, she refers to her earlier conflict as "my awful time of uncertainty."

Colleen Keller of Colorado Springs, Colorado, found herself hitting the same ball from the opposite court: "My daughter is six and this fall she'll be in first grade. I'm getting very restless and feel like I need to make a decision soon as to whether or not I should go back to

---

*As a mother at home myself for the past seventeen years, I believe in mothers at home and am glad I have been one. At the same time, I am very proud of the progress which women have made in the "out-of-the-home" world over the past several years.*

*People come in many wonderful varieties and with many varied feelings, experiences, understandings, and dreams. Many who would love to be at home with their children like us are single and childless. Many others are economically unable to stay home with their children though that would be their choice. Others of course have simply chosen to juggle career and child care as successfully as possible, and though that is not our choice, it is a position which we must also respect. If we all pull together, there are many ways in which we can help each other to make life better and more meaningful for us all.*

*I feel that I am a very privileged and very fortunate person to be having this beautiful experience of really knowing my children, sharing and helping them with their plans and dreams, and just being there when needed. The events of each day may not seem so big and important but when you add them all up, they are life itself. In short, I'm making a plea that we affirm ourselves up to the maximum, but that we do it in a very positive way which also demands of us an affirmation and acceptance of all of life.*

*Lora Rinker, Arlington, Virginia*

---

work full-time then. I've been very fortunate to be home with her since her birth. Yet I see how hard my husband works, and the never-ending bills don't seem to ever disappear. I know a second paycheck would help out tremendously and ease the burden off my husband's shoulders."

However, Colleen was worried about the effect such a lifestyle would have on her family. She pondered, "No more quiet moments during the day with my daughter, dinner wouldn't be ready when [my husband] walked in the door, I'd miss a lot of school functions. I have some serious decisions to make this summer."

Colleen reported to a new job as a secretary that fall, which she enjoys and plans to keep. Explaining that her salary will finally make possible the purchase of their first home, she observes, "I feel good knowing I spent seven years at home with my daughter. But occasionally I question whether I have done the right thing, and I'm not ruling out the possibility that I may not always want to work."

The feelings expressed by Antoinette and Colleen are not limited to mothers who are thinking of quitting or starting jobs. Even mothers who cannot or do not want to reconsider their choices feel threatened when they hear what they "ought" to be doing instead.

For example, Loretta Brooks, of Wenatchee, Washington, has been home with her two daughters for ten years and has no desire ever to work outside the home. Nevertheless, she is bothered by the "pressure to get 'out there' and get a job skill." Explaining that she and her husband have been careful to arrange life insurance that would provide for their family if anything should happen to the sole wage earner, Loretta laments the unsettling feelings created by those who say she should work:

"I love being at home. I have so many projects and hobbies. And I feel organizing and running a home are a full-time job. I also feel

---

*Bravo! Full-time mothers are very much underrated and discriminated against. I am, unfortunately, a working mother who commutes fifty miles each way. I have an eighteen-month-old son and plan another but am holding off for a while. It is very hard to have a young child and leave for work at 5:45 a.m. It is very difficult to find top-grade child care, particularly in a rural area, and find agreeable hours, too. I have been accused of being an "intense" mother. I do feel very frustrated concerning my need to work.*

*A government employee in Haymarket, Virginia*

fortunate that I don't have to seek outside work — I feel I am doing the most important job in the world. [Yet] in the back of my mind is the nagging self-doubt — maybe I just stay at home because I couldn't make it anywhere else!

"When I was growing up, I just wanted to be married and have a family. But society makes you feel anyone could do that! Is it wrong to love creating homes that provide a haven of peace and care — really a rare thing these days?"

Meanwhile, a working mother of two sons in Charlotte, North Carolina, wrote us about the hurt many women who must work experience when they encounter suggestions that young children need a mother at home. This mother found herself facing a divorce without a sufficient income to support herself and her boys. She had been home since the birth of her first child and desperately fought the idea of leaving him and his younger brother in someone else's care while she went off each day to make a living.

Searching for a job she never wanted was frightening, and orienting her two-year-old son to a routine he disliked was heartwrenching — especially when she was still wrestling with the other crises and trauma associated with divorce. When she did indeed survive that tortuous year, succeeding in both the acquisition of a good job and the smooth adjustment of a sensitive little boy to a day-care center, she needed praise for surmounting the problems in her life, not criticism for "abandoning" her sons.

"There is a big thing about facing what is demanded and finding one's way through it and trying very hard to feel okay about it," she explains, referring to a certain pride she developed to see herself through her ordeal. "In the face of having to find a place for yourself in the paying work force, and [then] carving out that place — despite

---

*My husband and I both felt it important that I quit my full-time teaching position in order to stay home with our two young children and teach them the values and principles that we consider important. With most of my friends in the work force, and after paging through countless magazines dealing with working mothers, I sometimes found myself feeling inferior for deciding to stay home.*

*[After reading about your group] I felt relieved to discover that there are other mothers who feel strongly about staying at home, and are willing to speak out about it.*

*Kathy Davis, Belleville, Michigan*

---

the fact that you're not an ambitious 'career' woman and didn't prepare yourself academically to earn money, and despite the real competition from all those young, upwardly mobile and ambitious 'kids' — you need to feel proud when you do overcome these obstacles. It did feel good when I was able to pay those damn bills!!" But she remembers, "I used to do arithmetic every day to see if I could find a way to pay bills and be home." And so, much unhappiness — even anger — surfaces when she reads articles about being home which "reinforce the belief I have that I cannot act upon" and "paint a picture of a life I'm not able to lead with my boys."

## Guilt Takes Many Forms

The feelings described above, which are primarily defensive reactions to any mention of "the other choice," represent only the most obvious of many forms of guilt. Today, both mothers who stay at home and mothers who enter the work force full-time face a whole range of guilt feelings unique to each situation. For example, mothers who work might appear to have the general support of society. Yet this supposed endorsement of their choice offers little consolation when they are beset by the constant frustration of feeling needed in two places at the same time. For example, a mother from Michigan, who was widowed when her son was an infant and spent several years as a single working mother, asks, "How many times can you call in and say, 'I won't be in — my child is sick' before you don't have a job any more?"

Some other less obvious conflicts which result in feelings of guilt have been described to us by many working mothers:

• I feel guilty when I have to accept less than the best child care arrangements.

• I feel guilty when I miss school events or when I don't have the time to volunteer as often as I think I should.

---

*I'm a mom who loves staying home to raise my son, but [I] have to return to work out of financial need. I'm certain we will cope just fine with the situation.*

*I think women today need a lot of support from each other based upon whatever decision they make regarding the raising of children. We live in a very complex world and should join together rather than criticize each other for choices we make.*

*J.B., Southfield, Michigan*

---

• I feel guilty when I end up using my "quality time" hours of the evening and weekend to do routine household chores and errands.

• I feel guilty when the house isn't spotless, the laundry isn't done, and the cookies aren't homemade.

By the same token, mothers who are at home full-time also admit to a variety of guilt feelings which cause periodic fears that they should perhaps seek employment outside the home. Some of the feelings most often expressed by mothers at home are these:

*I feel guilty leaving the entire responsibility to meet the family's financial obligations to my husband.*

In many areas of the country, it is truly difficult to avoid financial stress with a single source of income. Although mothers who stay home are sometimes painted as leisure-class women who play tennis while their husbands make a healthy (even wealthy) income, most of the women who write to us certainly do not maintain any such lifestyle. Rather, they speak of sacrificing not only "extras," but necessities as well. They observe the financial pressures placed on their husbands and feel a desire to share the load.

Betsy Carlson, a mother from Kingwood, Texas, intended to go back to work after a three-month maternity leave. She ended up at home because, "I found an overwhelming love for my child, child care options that made me cry, and the fact that the baby was keeping me plenty busy and tired." However, she found it took "many months to overcome the feelings that I was just being 'lazy' and the

---

*I am the mother of a three-year-old girl who has chosen to put my teaching career "on hold" and stay at home with her (and any other children we hope to be blessed with) during these all-important early years. I constantly read that I am part of a "dying breed" — that what I've chosen to do is "out-of-date and unfulfilling," that it's not as important as having a "real job." I can't tell you how happy it makes me to know there are others like me who are indeed "alive and well" and enjoy what we choose to do.*

*I became a teacher because I do love children. I wanted to be part of influencing the future of our country and I felt I could do a great job in the classroom. But my child (and future children) are even more important and I wanted to be responsible for building their characters and shaping their personalities on a day-to-day, moment-by-moment basis — something that can only be done with me being at home during the day. I have received great support from my husband, but it's terrific to know there are other women who believe as I do.*

*Diane E. Poliseno, Lake View, New York*

---

guilt of putting all the financial burden of the household on my husband."

Many mothers find ways to supplement their partners' salary by taking on part-time work or by earning money from home. Others learn to redirect portions of their limited income by inventing creative methods to save money. Also, it is not uncommon for mothers on slim budgets to point out that going to work full-time can actually cost a family so much money (in child care, transportation, etc.) that its economic advantages pale next to the emotional disadvantages. Still, many mothers continue to feel guilty for not bringing in half the family income.

### I feel guilty for not using my education.

No other generation of women has entered the childbearing years with so much formal education behind it. Because a college degree was so meaningful to our parents' generation, we often had access to the best schooling their money could buy. Their willingness to sacrifice so that we could obtain better opportunities in the job market was obvious to us in our younger years and remains vivid in our minds today.

In the great majority of cases, however, that prized education had a very specific purpose. The kinds of degrees we sought prepared us for a fairly narrow range of activities. Overnight, motherhood thrust us into an entirely different world, where equations, treatises, and expert opinions (even on the subject of childrearing!) did amazingly little to solve our immediate problems. Worse yet, mothering and keeping current in our former fields of endeavor, if we have learned to do it all, is rarely achieved without several months — or years — of trial and error. No wonder so many mothers feel guilty about ex-

---

*My wife received her degree in mathematics in 1970. She has chosen to stay at home to raise our four children (three, six, eight, and twelve).*

*Over the years she has received subtle criticism for her decision (even from me). However, her reasons have nothing to do with her aversion to "go to work." In fact, she is involved with many "out of home" projects. Her reasons are simply her priority to our children.*

*I would appreciate more information on your organization for two reasons. Primarily, I believe my wife has made the right choice and your organization affirms her decision. Secondarily, (this is hard to write!) you have a lot to say to people like me.*

*George R. Heron, Essexville, Michigan*

changing a job which depended on that valuable education for one that appears to leave it on the shelf to gather dust.

"After months of thought, I finally made the 'big' decision and tendered my resignation at work," writes Jan Treinen from Scottsdale, Arizona. "It took a lot of courage for me to do that. I had always been brought up and was educated to pursue that 'career!' I was even afraid to tell my parents for fear that they would feel my degree in business administration would be wasted. When I finally did tell them, at first it was met with doubts, then gradually was accepted when they realized how very much being at home means to me."

A mother of a preschool daughter who lives in the New York City area describes similar concerns she felt after coming home: "I hold a master's degree in secondary education and realize that I have so much to offer my daughter. Recently, though, I have begun to feel that the role of 'housewife' did not become someone who had spent eighteen years in preparation for a career. I knew the importance of a consistent mother figure during the early years of development and had experienced the rewards of teaching, but was ashamed to admit that I was a housewife." Only after a period of serious doubting did this mother come to realize "that what I am doing is something I have chosen to do. It is as important — if not more important — than any outside career."

*I feel guilty that I am not contributing something "important" to society.*

Society surely stands indicted by the number of mothers who stay home full-time who have at one time or another questioned the value of their work. A great majority of the women who write to us feel great sorrow over how little society respects the work they do. Linda Hand, a mother from Detroit, Michigan, who quit a seven-year career as a legal secretary to stay home with her son, recently told us, "At times I feel guilty because I actually enjoy being home, having my own schedule (after years of someone else making my schedule), being outside, and doing what I please." From Arcadia, California, Donne Davis writes: "After earning my master's degree in speech

---

*I worked for thirteen years prior to giving birth to my son last March. I enjoy being home so much but feel guilty and lonely compared to my friends who work full-time.*

*Marilyn Connell, Mesquite, Texas*

---

pathology, I worked for two years, then retired to stay home and raise my two children. I wouldn't be honest if I didn't admit to having many doubts over the past decade when I questioned my choice and wondered whether I was contributing enough to society by 'just caring for my family.'"

This feeling can be intensified for women who do not struggle financially to stay home. Kathleen Kane, a mother of two in Bethesda, Maryland, notes: "Because we can easily afford my not working, I feel sometimes as if it just looks like I'm being 'lazy' staying home — since it doesn't take any big financial sacrifice — one that would *prove* my dedication to the belief of staying home with my children. Having money does not make a woman's choices or her feelings about herself that much easier!"

Some women describe experiences in which they have not only felt condemned for "not contributing to society," but have actually been accused of taking from society without giving anything back. "At fifty-one, I have six 'children' ages twelve through twenty-eight and have seen mothering at home go from the expected to the tolerated to the actually antagonized position it holds today," writes Louise Biemer from Tampa, Florida. "I have even been called a 'parasite' for remaining at home in recent years."

### I feel guilty for letting down the women's movement.

For women who have fought their way up a traditionally male career ladder, abandoning positions that were not easily achieved can be traumatic — especially where a condescending "Why-should-I-hire-you-when-you'll-just-get-pregnant?" approach had to be conquered along the way. When a woman in such a situation does finally leave work to be home with her children, she can feel tremendous guilt at having "proven the boss right," thereby making the climb in that company even more difficult for the women who come behind her.

Holly Coyne, a mother of three in McLean, Virginia, understands this kind of guilt. She had always wanted children, but spent the first seven years of her marriage struggling with an apparent infertility problem while she worked. Because of an interest in finance, she eventually went back to school for an MBA degree, and just after graduation found out she was pregnant. Torn over whether to stay home or go on in a field in which she now had invested quite a bit of time and money, she decided to go ahead with her career. When she began applying for jobs, she was almost six months pregnant.

Holly recalls, "I was hired by the largest bank in town, after being told by several others to come back after the baby was born. I loved working there. They supported me through two children." Yet after her second maternity leave, Holly quit her job to move to another state. She has not yet decided when she will return to her career. "To some extent I feel I let down the women's movement," she muses. "I felt I owed them a lot because I knew my job had been made possible by women who previously fought for their rights. And there were an awful lot of women in training when I left."

## Every Mother Feels the Pressure to Work

Mothers who enter the outside workplace and mothers who remain at home have more in common than a mutual lack of support from society. They also agree that the pressure for a woman to hold a job during the childrearing years is extreme and far outweighs the few voices promoting mothering at home. And, in general, mothers are truly resentful of this pressure. The depth of anger felt by some is evident in this letter from a mother in Michigan:

"I worked fifty-five hours a week at a drug warehouse making $5.72 an hour, plus overtime. But I *never really worked* until my two children came along, fourteen months apart. I love them. I want to support and nurture them. I gave up a good income to do so. I didn't want strangers raising my kids. Still don't.

"But why do I feel compelled to 'go out and work for a living?' What am I doing now — playing? I'm not a 'dumb housewife.' I'm a full-time, hardworking, often exhausted mother and wife who thinks my kids need me.

"Why should I, or we, be put down for tending our country's most precious resources — our children? It's high time we speak up for a job with long hours, low pay, and no respect. When people ask me if I work, I say, 'You're darn right I work — I work hard at a challenging job. I just don't get a paycheck.'"

The pressures are so great that women who feel they had no trouble making rational decisions at other crossroads in their lives find themselves swayed and torn and wearied over the "work versus home" issue and still unable to find a comfortable answer. Susan Piancenza, a professional psychologist from Madison, Wisconsin, indicates that even several years experience advising others has not helped her come up with a satisfactory solution for herself: "Although I returned to work after a year's maternity leave — and only work half-time — I still am seriously considering being a full-time mother at home. But I need support! It seems that most literature today respects and supports the woman who 'does it all' (career, family, and loving relationship with spouse). Even though I have a master's degree in counseling and have worked in the field for six years, I find it impossible to counsel myself and difficult to re-frame my self-concept to exclude work outside the home where so many people put the value."

Writes Susan Danielson, a mother of two in New Orleans, Louisiana, who works part-time as a math instructor at a local university: "I often feel hopelessly torn between my requirements for motherhood and my requirements for a career. The media shoves 'having it all' down our throats. I need to see another side." In a letter from Nashua, New Hampshire, Judy Lindquist relates, "I was born and raised during the women's movement. As a teen, a young adult, a college student, and a newlywed, I was bombarded with the media hype about today's woman 'having it all' — husband, children, home, and career. If all these 'other' women could have it all, then so could I! I planned to continue [my career but] it is simply not possible to give 100% to everything — there is not enough of one human being to go around. We must make choices, and something has to suffer."

In addition to society's pressure to work, many women endure a more exhausting kind of pressure from family and friends. Sometimes it is even initiated by husbands, who in turn bear both social and economic pressure to have a wife who works. Writes one mother from Salt Lake City, Utah: "It gets very lonely sometimes, and the pressure to 'toss in the apron' can get heavy when all of your close friends and relatives work and think you are nuts for staying at home. I have three wonderful children, ages sixteen, fourteen, and three. At least they are supportive and encouraging, as is their father. But he gets pressure at work, too, to have me work — with statements like, 'How can you let her just sit around and live off you?'" And from a mother in New York we hear: "I don't receive any support from anyone with my commitment to staying home. My husband, who makes enough income to support us all, wants an additional income from me for the luxuries one doesn't allow. My own mother worked all her life in a factory and ran the household, and can't understand why I can't do both as well."

Such pressure makes it difficult for a woman to stand by her choice, and often results in unhappiness — whether she stays home as she desires or goes to work to please others. A mother from St. Paul, Minnesota relates:

"After years of applying for various jobs because of a guilty conscience (and failing miserably at most), I've finally settled comfortably into housekeeping and caring for my two daughters, ages five and one. I suffered a nervous breakdown and a four-month-long hospitalization period before I finally came to grips with the need to do what I wanted, not what my mother and husband believed I should do.

"Walking several children home the other day, I realized with sudden clarity that I was truly happy. I no longer make excuses — my children are lovely and well-tempered now that I'm no longer going through the agonies of trying to teach, complete a graduate degree, and maintain a home. I'm happy, and my husband is learning to accept that I do contribute to this family even if it isn't in always tangible terms."

Certainly, the effort it takes to overcome the pressure to go to work is often overlooked. Perhaps it is best expressed by a mother from Illinois: "Although I grew up in the rural Midwest, in a home that preached and practiced equality, the choice to work at home was somehow less than equal — at least in my mind. Ironically, it has taken all of my feminism and activism to find the place where I can parent and be content with my decision — that place is home."

## Exchanging One Socially Imposed Role for Another

Much has been said and written about the progress of women in the decades since Betty Friedan's landmark book, *The Feminine Mystique.* Indeed, we have seen women welcomed in a broader range of professions; we have witnessed greater awareness of women's talents; we have exulted in the demise of the "dumb blonde" image; and we have applauded widespread attempts to combat rape and spouse abuse. There is certainly much to be grateful for and much that the younger of our generation already take for granted because they do not remember or relate to a time when it was any other way.

Yet the claims that women have broken free of severe social constraints and expectations are simply not true. Our role is as clearly defined as it was a century ago. Only its character has changed — and the face of the people who promote it.

Where once we were "expected" to be at home, today we are "expected" to be at work. Where once we felt compelled to sacrifice ourselves in the interest of our families, we are now being urged to sacrifice our families while we "look out for Number One."

♦        ♦        ♦

Certainly, women will never be completely unfettered as long as our lives are spent fighting or fitting roles defined for us by someone else. Whether a tradition that says women belong in the kitchen or a media that says we belong in the workplace, such expectations will continue to rob us until we quit reacting and start purposefully charting a course of our own.

*Part II*

# Startling Realizations and Gentle Discoveries

*Chapter 3*

# Startling Realizations and Gentle Discoveries...
# ... About Our Children

No parenting textbook, no childbirth preparation class, no well-meaning advice from relatives and friends can prepare a woman for even the first few moments of motherhood. As soon as the newborn child — soft, wrinkled, and shockingly alive — is placed in a mother's arms, her world is permanently altered in ways she will continue to discover daily for the rest of her life.

None of us has exactly the same reaction to mothering. For some, nurturing is second nature from the start, as if the springwater of maternal instincts suddenly bubbled forth from an unknown source hidden deep within. For others, it is like adopting a creature from outer space who neither communicates nor comprehends by conventional methods, who nevertheless expects fulfillment of every demand.

There are too many such variables in this line of work for any mother to anticipate ever identifying a "right" way to do the job. The most alike among us will face differences in personality, in health, and in environment; differences in economic situations, in family crises, and in daily habits and routines. Still, for all the gradations of circumstances and feelings that separate one mother's experiences from another's, the variations are almost always variations on a theme. There seems to be, within the general realm of motherhood, a lot of common ground.

This common ground is not unlike that earned by soldiers who have gone to war. There may be great differences in what any two soldiers have actually seen and done; differences in how they reacted under the pressures of battle. They have fought in different countries, even in different wars. But they both have witnessed human strivings and sufferings of unusual proportions; they have shared, though not necessarily together, the unveiling of a certain unique perspective on life. They can speak together with inferences they know the other will understand which they would never use with someone who hadn't fought a war.

Mothers, like soldiers, have a common frame of reference unique to mothers, which should put them at ease in each other's company, which should allow them to begin a relationship on a shade different level than could two other total strangers. However, this shared vista of motherhood does not automatically result in a sisterhood for many mothers. Like anything that forces us to reach deep within our own souls, our feelings about motherhood are often difficult to identify

---

*My husband and I are the proud parents of nine great children from the ages of twenty-three down to eight. I have been an "at-home mom" for twenty-four years — what a blessing and joy!*

*Last November, I was really having a down period due to the fact that new moms had moved onto our street. One is a medical doctor and the other a flight attendant. They had little children and were also working full-time in their chosen professions, and here I was, an at-home, full-time mom, and really not keeping up with doing all that in my mind I wanted to do.*

*At Thanksgiving break, as our twenty-two-year-old daughter, Michelle, and I visited, I shared with her my feelings. She was simply the medicine that I needed to hear that day. She responded, "But, Mom, I would not be where I am today had you not been where you were! You were my support system, my encourager, my peace, and my challenger to go for it and to use my talents. You were always there to point out my special, God-given talents so that I could reflect upon them and put them into use!"*

*I thought all of you young moms would enjoy hearing these words. Our nine children are all really great. We now have six teenagers and they all are serious students but also have the concern and kindness for their fellow travelers in this life. We have three in college and they are truly the lighted candle in some very dark areas.*

*So I encourage all of you moms to stay with this blessed of all jobs . . . [your children] will grow in the environment of love and care that nourishes the heart and spirit, and know that they are truly special children of God and important in your daily life.*

*Elizabeth A. Beaulaurier, Burlingame, California*

---

About Our Children

and express — particularly in a society which rarely pauses to consider inclinations of the heart.

Yet many mothers long for the comfort of an empathetic comradeship. We have chosen, therefore, to devote the following pages to the clarification of some of the most universally shared feelings about mothering, especially mothering at home.

## No One Told Me I Would Feel This Way About My Child

Motherhood catches almost everyone by surprise. Indeed by its very nature, it is not the sort of activity for which we can train in advance. Most mothers eventually find they have relied on preconceived notions about what motherhood will be like that, for the most part, were destined to dissolve. But it is one thing to admit our own naivete when we realize our misconceptions were based on inexperience, and quite another to feel we were misled.

The pervasive Do-Something-More-Important-With-Your-Life philosophy of today leaves too many young women unprepared for the dramatic changes a child's presence brings to anyone's life. And more and more first-time mothers, astounded at the strength of the emotional ties they feel for their infants, are accusing the society that educated them: "Why didn't anyone tell me I would feel this way about my child?"

In an age when we are told that good mothering is just a matter of finding the right sitter and learning to arrange "quality time," most of us could never have envisioned how completely we would be taken in by these delicious miniature people. We had no concept of the bonding power of total trust, unconditional love, and happy, inno-

---

*I have been working at home since our twin boys joined our family five and a half years ago. Recently, a little girl joined our family and I find my present job of raising children far more mentally challenging than the nine years I worked as a nurse.*

*Rita Anderson, Rockville, Maryland*

*I'm a woman who has always wanted to stay at home with children (in spite of, or because of?!, a very rich educational background). Until we had a beautiful, healthy, and very colicky baby six months ago, I never appreciated the extraordinary talent, humor, and patience mothers at home need to develop to stay sane, creative, and happy.*

*Eileen Beery Noble, Minneapolis, Minnesota*

---

cent dependence, especially when such qualities radiate from someone who looks like family and doesn't know life can be any other way.

For women who plan on spending a long time getting to know their newborns, especially those who plan to stay home, the depth of feeling they experience for their children is a pleasant surprise. But for many new mothers who honestly believed they could simply locate the perfect sitter and glide smoothly back into life as before, the truth can be devastating. No one warns us that we might not *want* to leave our babies.

Kathy Miller Rindock, of Allentown, Pennsylvania, wrote to us:

"We spoke about the conflict of mothers [like me] who, before the birth of their first child, naively assumed they knew what they wanted to be when they grew up — a SUPERMOM! You know, that mythical creature in the pantyhose commercial — faster than a speeding toddler, more powerful than ring-around-the-collar, and able to leap across the board meetings in a single bound.

"Then you have that carefully planned child and WHAMMO! You first gaze into those unfocused blue eyes, feel the caress of that downy head against your breast, breathe the sweet smell of *your* baby, and everything you've believed in and fought for all these years goes right up in smoke because . . . you don't want to go back to work. You can't even conceive of separating yourself from that tiny miracle nestled in your arms."

Pam Svoboda from McCook, Nebraska, had a similar experience. "I had no doubt I would go back to work after the baby was born," she told us. "Throughout all nine months of pregnancy I assured every-

---

*I am at home with five-and-a-half-year-old triplets and a four-and-a-half-year-old singleton. When I was expecting triplets, I looked forward to quitting work and had planned on staying home even if I had only expected one first baby. But I got three! Financially, we would not have been ahead if we paid for day-care for four and I went back to work. I felt it was impossible.*

*I am very glad to be home with my kids and feel we all would miss a lot if I were working. Even though my husband hears the day's events when he comes in the door at night, he misses a lot. I don't want to. I feel it's very important to be here when needed — be it for my discipline or to share the excitement of, "Mom! Look what I did!"*

*Louella Heitman, Menomonee Falls, Wisconsin*

one that I was not a 'homebody,' that I'd be bored at home, and that I needed to be out in the world. Then she was born. The nurse brought this small, soft, warm baby to me, and I immediately fell deeply in love. I had no idea she would be so special. I loved everything about her — her clenched fist, her rosebud mouth, her smell, her cry, and my heart felt it would burst with her smile."

## Economic Realities

Yet the strength of such feelings cannot erase hard economic facts for many women who truly expected to have no trouble leaving their children in day-care and who made no financial preparations to stay home. Both Kathy and Pam returned to their full-time jobs outside the home, Kathy with a great deal of resentment, Pam with full expectations of "adjusting" to working motherhood in a few weeks.

Pam, who went back to work as planned when her daughter was six weeks old, found herself spending work hours watching the clock and wondering what her baby was doing. She says: "It didn't take long to realize that what I really wanted was to be a full-time, twenty-four-hour-a-day mother. My heart was not in my job anymore. At first, I told myself I needed to give it more time and I would eventually adjust, but the more time I spent away from my baby the more I longed to be with her. I have never regretted the decision I made to stay home."

But for Kathy Rindock, staying home was not an immediate option. After her return to work, she began "scrimping and saving and planning to [come] home, at least part-time" by the end of the year. Several months later, as she relates it, "federal funding for my social

---

*I was the breadwinner for four years while my husband was in seminary. When he began working at his vocation, I began working at mine — being at home when our first child was born. We now have four children, and while it can get* real *crazy around here, this is where I belong.*

*My rewards have been in the form of the first steps, the first words, delighted peek-a-boo grins, and towers made of pots and pans and Tupperware containers. As my children get older, it's rewarding to help and watch as they learn to deal with problems and frustrations — with the tools I have offered them. Kids won't wait for "quality time" and weekends.*

*I'm so glad* Welcome Home *is showing what a formidable source remains in the home. To those on the fence — c'mon in, the water's fine!*

Nancy Waggener, Ashland, Wisconsin

work position was cut. I don't believe my caseworker at the unemployment office ever had a more cheerful client." Kathy was able to complete training as a consultant to a parent education group and begin working part-time.

Unfortunately, many mothers who must work may never have the opportunity to be home full-time with their children. A mother from Alligerville, New York, writes: "I'm a single parent supporting two children and, of course, I've been working outside my home for years. While I've been able to manage to be a working mother and still have time at home, the pressure is often more than I should have to bear. I've always held the hope that I could be an at-home mom, but as time goes by and my children get older, the prospect seems more distant than ever."

## The Real "Expert" on Rearing a Child
## Is a Loving Parent

For the mothers mentioned above, the desire to be home with their babies grew out of extraordinary feelings they had for their children from birth. For other mothers, the first months of caring for an infant are so overwhelming that their thoughts are turned not towards creating bonds, but fleeing from them. Sometimes a mother doesn't realize just how strongly she feels about the smallest details of her child's well-being until she goes back to work and entrusts her child to another's care. The following is Linda Burton's story.

---

# A Search for Child Care
### by Linda Burton

I hadn't intended to stay at home. I said I wasn't born for it. Having my first child at the age of thirty-three created an upheaval in my life unlike anything I had experienced.

Before the birth of my first child, I had been a professional full-time fund-raiser for a public-interest law firm. It was a harrowing job, sometimes, but it was fun and made good use of my energies. At the end of the day, I used to look forward to meeting my husband and friends somewhere in town. We would relax, catch up on the day's events, and generally enjoy each other.

After the birth of my first child, I found that I could no longer relax and celebrate the end of the day, because for the first time in my life, my days had no end. Rather frighteningly, the demands on my time and energy were suddenly whipped from my control by a baby who did not seem to care what time of day it was or how much sleep I had missed. Walking the floor with my child, knowing that he was keeping me from doing much that I really wanted to do, made me angry.

When my husband and I first discussed having children, we had no real idea how radically they would constrict our lifestyle. Like many other modern young couples, we had followed the dictates of Lamaze and LeBoyer. We had our baby by natural childbirth, spent hours "bonding" with our newborn, and never let him cry without picking him up. According to the new "parenting" books, we were teaching our son that his needs would be met, first thing in life.

But while my child didn't cry, I did. I missed my job and my friends; I felt poverty-stricken, and I looked awful. So, like many young women faced with the same predicament, I decided to go back to work.

Without too much trouble, I found a job writing for a public television station — and I happily set out to enjoy life once again. I assumed that I would simply give my child good "quality" time in the evenings and on weekends and, in the meantime, I would use all my energies to find an absolutely sterling person to care for him during the day.

I researched child care with a vengeance. Luckily, I did find someone to care for my son who seemed fine. She lasted a month. During that brief return to the office, however, I made some remarkable discoveries.

I discovered that I had no "quality" time for my child in the evening; indeed, I felt like I had no time at all. I was tired. Although I loved my son, and knew that he needed attention from me, somehow I was unable to give much of it after a day at the office.

I also discovered, to my surprise, that I missed my child when I was gone. I worried about how he was being dressed, fed, cared for. I worried that his bright inquisitiveness was being dulled by the housekeeper who, while a kind and decent person, lacked a certain intellectual vitality.

I was almost relieved when my housekeeper quit. I came back home to attend to my son and, again, searched for child care. Diligently, and over what came to be a period of two years, I searched for child care everywhere, from the local town newspaper to the best nanny schools in London.

Yet everywhere I looked, it always seemed like a long waiting list of mothers had been there before me. We commiserated with each other. Trying to find the "right" kind of full-time child care, we discovered, was a lot like trying to handicap a horserace or beat the roulette wheel at Las Vegas. No matter how many setbacks we had, we kept giving it one more try, holding out for what we knew was the intoxicating probability of an imminent lucky break. Whether the spoils of victory were unimaginable amounts of personal wealth or the babysitter popularized in legend who was kind, intelligent, put our children first, and never got sick, we fervently believed that there, but for a simple key to the right system, went us.

I remember the zeal with which a few mothers at work would guard their child care sources, passing on names of favored sitters to a select friend or two, with all the covert machinations of a Mata Hari. But no matter how closely kept were the names of the "really good" sitters which some mothers managed to stumble on, there always came that inevitable day when they lost them. Maybe one of them moved, maybe the sitter just got tired and decided to give up sitting for a while. Or maybe the mother simply decided that the "really good" sitter wasn't so "really good" after all. Whatever the reason, we all learned to pick ourselves up and begin searching again.

When I was looking hard for child care, I spent literally hours on the telephone, every day, trying to scout out the best available care. Other more broken-in mothers shared their allegedly foolproof "Lists of What to Ask Potential Housekeepers" who telephoned me in response to the many advertisements I placed. They suggested nefarious ways to tap into the market of illegal aliens (remarking that it would be nice to have someone who spoke English, but concluding that we couldn't have everything) and passed on whispered directions toward certain population groups who were rumored to "be wonderful with children."

## Nannies and Housekeepers

At the beginning, I confined my search for child care to housekeepers and nannies. However, no matter how much I wanted my child to have personal, one-on-one care and attention, provided in his own home, I always seemed to come up against one of the same three obstacles. First of all, nannies and housekeepers were very expensive, and their wages would have eaten up a major chunk of my salary. I soon learned that in conjunction with the other expenses of working outside the home — clothing, transportation, lunches, and the convenience foods which became almost essential for cooking — the expense of one-on-one care was something my husband and I could not reasonably handle.

Second, if the tedious progression of interviews which I conducted with the aspiring housekeepers who answered my ads was any indication of the sort of care givers available for hire in the nanny market, even the people able to afford full-time, one-on-one care were rarely getting what they bargained for. The truth of the matter was that an overwhelming percentage of the people who came to my door, ready and willing to care for my children, were clearly unqualified for the job.

Finally, I learned that nanny-housekeepers — no matter how good or how qualified — rarely stay around very long. A job, after all, is still a job, and even the most capable of nannies is not in the job for the long-run. For some reason, many of us nanny-seekers must have acquired vastly sentimentalized notions from old English history books or PBS television series that a typical nanny came to change the diapers and stayed on for the weddings. The reality was that few modern-day nannies stuck around long enough to see a baby move into toddlerhood. Even the most congenial and affluent of employers, who gave their nannies multiple gifts, lavish vacations, free cars, high wages, and desirable working conditions, frequently complained about the eternal search for "yet another" nanny.

## The Child Care Merry-Go-Round

This last problem, especially, seemed almost indigenous to every available kind of child care I located. Nannies seemed to come and go, as did family day-care providers, almost constantly; even the staffs of most day-care institutions, I learned, have a notoriously high turnover rate, while the outward serene appearance of the facility itself remains constant.

Although I would find myself joking about the on-again, off-again nature of the child care merry-go-round, I soon realized I was becoming uneasy about what this process was doing to my by-this-time two children. I knew there were people murmuring about how good all this upheaval must be for the children; I read about one woman who laughed that her daughter was "being raised by a committee." But she told herself that her daughter was getting to know a lot of people and was learning how to make rapid social adjustments.

Yet there was something else that I could see my own children learning, along with rapid social adjustment, which frightened me, no matter how lightly I dismissed its implications. I could see that it was unsettling and traumatic for them, once they had anchored their love, confidence, and trust in someone, to experience abandonment by them; and I feared that they were learning, in their own self-interest, not to invest too many of their feelings in other people, or to be willing to commit themselves to future long-term emotional relationships.

I wanted my children to learn that the people who cared for them would not leave them. While I knew my husband and I would not leave them, the fact remained that we were away at an office all day. We were not our children's primary care givers, no matter how much we liked to think of ourselves that way, and we could not in truth be relied upon to respond to their needs for the great majority of their waking hours. I was beginning to see that I wanted my children to have a reliable, consistent, loving person upon whom they could depend for guidance, who was available to them during much of their day — and that the status quo of musical babysitters wasn't going to give it to them.

## Family Day-Care

When the problems with hiring a nanny-housekeeper appeared insurmountable, I decided to go ahead and give family-centered day-care a try. Initially, this home-based care seemed like an attractive option to me because I assumed that my children would be in a cozy, homey atmosphere during the day, placed with a relatively small group of children, who could be nice playmates for them. And family day-care had the added happy bonus of being much more affordable than one-on-one care. Yet my high hopes rose — and predictably fell again — with each successive experience in home-based care.

It seemed that one of the biggest and most consistent problems I encountered with family day-care was rampant over-crowding. Although I noticed that local governments were frequently trying to regulate the numbers of children allowed in any one day-care home at the same time, I could also see that those regulations were increasingly caving in to public pressure for "more child care." And the regulations were very difficult to enforce. Time and again, I left my children in the care of a sitter who assured me she cared for "very few" children, only to return on an impromptu visit to find staggering numbers of "drop-ins" had joined the "very few."

Another problem I found with family day-care homes was that the care givers generally were women who wanted very much to stay home with their own children, but who took in extra children to help supplement the family income. I found that it was next to impossible, in a situation like that, to expect the sitter to put the needs of my children first. Naturally, even the kindest and best-intentioned person in the world would respond to her own children more quickly and more sensitively than to the children of a relative stranger. And I would frequently see my children, no matter how subtly, come to perceive themselves in an inferior, less-favored position than "Johnny and Rachel" or "Mary Beth."

Third, on visits to family day-care homes, I was surprised at the number of times I observed a sitter relating to my children differently from the way I would have done: from how she responded to a request for an apple, to where she put them down for a nap, to attempts to deal with (or ignore) conflicts and questions. Too frequently, I found myself observing a sitter and uneasily reflecting, "I wouldn't do it that way!" This is not to say, please understand, that I always believed my way was the "right" way; not at all. But I was surprised at the large number of clear opinions I appeared to have about some of the smallest things that were a part of my children's everyday lives.

I came to see that the raising of a child did not represent simple custodial upkeep. Rather, my children were learning lessons, making choices, and being guided by the repetition of small human interchanges. The largest decisions about the direction of their future, I was learning, were made in the course of these apparently inconsequential daily interchanges. Here, they would most indelibly implant information about their perceived place in the world, their relation to other people, and the value they placed in themselves, in their own potential and their own goodness.

Last, I discovered that family day-care by its very "cozy" nature is invisible and anonymous and therefore subject to astonishing abuse. When I was at the office, I did not in fact ever really KNOW what went on with my children during the day. Oh, I could draw certain inferences, based on the way my children behaved when I picked them up at day's end, but my inferences were incorrect on enough occasions to warrant my pulling the children out of family day-care altogether. Honest information about the realities of a child's day in a day-care situation is not always easy to come by. The day-care provider has an obvious vested interest in presenting the rosiest picture possible. Like many children left in family day-care, my youngest couldn't talk at all; and I suspected his older brother might be easily intimidated or bullied into not talking. Given an unhappy day-care situation, I could see how my children might well have assumed — since they had no reference point — that their unhappiness was a simple part of their existence.

Also, I am embarrassed to say that there were far too many days when I just did not want to HEAR about what my children did during the day, how they were treated, and so on. I would leave work harassed, tired, frustrated, and eager to put dinner on the table, and I did not want additional "problems" from my children. It became easy to overlook an unpleasant or unacceptable day-care situation simply because it became one burden too many to handle.

In actual practice, I never found an accurate way to evaluate the merit of a day-care situation. Despite my most painstaking investigations, many environments that appeared loving and constructive on initial (and sometimes repeated) examination, turned out later to be something quite different.

In one instance, I found the "absolutely marvelous" family day-care provider, recommended by trusted friends, sleeping on her sofa while eleven children (she had informed me that she only cared for five children) wandered aimlessly around in front of the blaring TV. Another time, on an unannounced visit, I found that the "highly recommended" licensed day-care provider confined seven preschoolers to her tiny dining room. I found them huddled together, leaning over a barricade to watch a TV program showing in the adjacent room.

Such disappointing — sometimes horrifying — child care stories clearly differed from mother to mother, but the general theme, I learned, remained the same. It seemed that no matter how many checklists I consulted, visits I made, or references I checked, my conclusion never varied. No one was going to make the loving care and welfare of my children a priority but me.

## Institutional Day-Care

At one point, in spite of a prejudice against it, I even investigated institutional day-care for my children. I talked to a number of mothers who regularly used day-care, and I read the literature of many of the new day-care chains located near my home. I was offended by much of the public relations language in the day-care brochures which came my way — language which attempted to soothe my anxieties and dispel my guilt at the notion of leaving my children in institutional care — but language which also denied the instincts of my heart and my down-home common sense. Many of the brochures even seemed to claim that they could do a better, more "educated" and professional job of raising my children than I could.

So when I checked out the possibilities of institutional care for my own children, I was dismayed at what I found: The people staffing many child care institutions certainly weren't the superior, kind and loving, multiply-degreed maternal paragons which the day-care brochures had touted. Many of the people I saw on the staffs of our child care institutions, on the contrary, were under-paid, under-educated, and under-interested.

This is not to say, of course, that I did not find some superb, dedicated day-care directors. During my search for child care, I spoke with some of them at great length. In fact, I became somewhat irritated as they tried, with great feeling, both to convince me that they were not the best thing for my children and to help me come up with ways to work from home so I could be with my children. At the end of one phone conversation with a day-care director, I was rather taken aback to hear her finally sigh, "If you really must have some other kind of care for your children, I suppose we're the best; but your care would be the best of all."

I disagreed. I still believed that there was a babysitter out there with my name on her and all I had to do was beat the right bush — find the right system — that would bring her out of hiding. In time, however, my exhaustive and intense search for child care taught me this critical lesson: No matter how many licenses we issue or inspections we require, no matter how rigid the guidelines we establish or how much money we pay, we must one day face the fact that it is impossible to have quality controls over the capacity of one human being to love and care for another.

And all of a sudden, the notion occurred to me that perhaps the elusive, almost mystical "she" was not out there. After all, here we were, millions of women trying to hire someone warm, wonderful, motherly, and loving. All of a sudden, common sense told me that there simply weren't enough warm, wonderful, motherly, and loving people to go around. And even if they *were* out there, it was clear that they didn't want to give priority attention to *my* children. They wanted to take care of their own children.

While I — and most of my friends — were saying our minds were "too good" to stay at home and raise our children, none of

◆
◆
◆
◆
◆
◆
◆
◆
◆
◆
◆
◆
◆
◆

us ever asked the question, "Then what sort of minds *should* be raising our children — minds that were *not* very good?"

My carefully worded advertisements for child care literally came back to haunt me. I was looking for someone "loving, tender, reliable, responsible, nurturing, intelligent, and resourceful." I had wanted someone with a driver's license, good English, a sense of fun, and an alert, lively manner. I wanted someone who would encourage my children's creativity, take them on interesting outings, answer all their little questions, and rock them to sleep. I wanted someone who would be a "part of the family."

Slowly, painfully, after really thinking about what I wanted for my children and rewriting advertisement after advertisement, I came to the stunning realization that the person I was looking for was right under my nose. I had been desperately trying to hire me.

## Nurturing Children Is Much More Challenging and Demanding Than I Was Led to Believe

Most of us remember those cozy evenings before we had children when we would sit around with our husbands discussing our plans for the next several years. We would bat around ideas about travel, different jobs, and new homes, figuring that the children we hoped to have would just somehow "fit in" to our lives. And if there was any doubt about how they would fit in, we would shrug it off, saying, "We'll just bring them along with us." It was easy, in those uncomplicated days, to treat our as-yet-unborn children as the parentheses in the otherwise fascinating narrative of our life stories.

Yet, we were soon to discover that our first child often did not slide quite so neatly into the prepared pockets of our lives. Most of us didn't know anything about babies. We may have known how to meet deadlines at work and negotiate the subway system, but we didn't know how to change diapers or quiet a baby's tears. And in the beginning, many of us thought this sort of custodial upkeep was all there was to mothering. Only as we nurtured this little stranger day after day did it begin to dawn on us just how intellectually demanding mothering could be.

While some friends ask why we "waste" our education at home, many of us feel that mothering is the first job we've ever had that really uses all our education — both formal and informal. Connie

Cebulski de Perez, an American citizen living in Venezuela, remarks, "I am greatly offended by the assumption that all of my education is being wasted while I stay at home raising children. I have had to read and study so much about raising children since I became a mother." Connie, who acquired an "extensive educational background" before the births of her four sons, and who worked in public accounting and banking where her managerial positions often forced her to deal with sensitive personnel problems, also notes, "I am utilizing all of my liberal arts background, my business administration specialty, my auditing perseverance, and my managerial experience to help my children."

Like Connie, many mothers are surprised to find out that mothering is a rather sophisticated endeavor — one which involves dealing on a daily basis with immensely complex and constantly evolving little beings. Every time we turn around there is someone new where a familiar child once stood. Suddenly we see that he has a sense of humor, that she loves horses, that he can reason deductively, that she is a budding leader; and we have to adjust our vision — and harder still, our actions — to match the latest assessment of their needs.

We never realized how much of a child's well-being later in life would depend on our woefully inadequate wisdom early in his life. Around every corner is a wonderful discovery — or an uncomfortable realization. We thrill at our new-found ability to cause a sunrise of understanding to burst upon a baffled three-year-old face. We shrink from the task ahead when we observe a child acting "just like me" — knowing that, for his sake, we must change ourselves before we can even think of changing him.

The weight of our new responsibility frightens us, fascinates us, overwhelms us. For this nurturing of children is not only a grander

---

*Our four sons are now grown and to say there were not days I now put in the "lost" file of my memory would not be true. But, there are far more that I remember with fondness — great fondness. So do the boys! My three daughters-in-law have each told me how their husbands have related stories of their childhood activities: walks, story hours, picnics, cookie-making sessions, "field trips," and so on.*

*Extended families were in the Midwest; hence, no grandmothers, aunts, cousins, etc., to offer a helping hand. Good friends and I exchanged sitting, shared clothes, ideas, tears, and laughs. Continue to enjoy the children.*

*A.E. Reidy, Towson, Maryland*

---

and more demanding work than we presumed; it is as bewildering as Alice's descent into Wonderland, in spite of the millions of people who have passed this way before. No matter the degree of our competence in a hundred other pursuits, every one of us is mothering in Braille, feeling our way from day to day, from month to month, from year to year.

## Time Is an Important Factor in a Child's Life

With lifestyles as busy as they are today, many of us share a genuine concern about the amount of time we give our children. Is it enough? we wonder. Do we spend it wisely? Linda Burton recalls the kind of time that was important to her when she was a child.

## *In Praise of Simmering*

### by Linda Burton

During my annual bout of the post-holiday blues, my mother decided to cheer me up by inviting the family to dinner. She also intended, she told me on the phone, to use the occasion to "christen" her new microwave oven.

Yes. My mother — a woman of some sixty-odd years — would dare to roast a stuffed chicken in fifteen new-fangled minutes of blazingly modern technological glory. I didn't like the idea.

To my mind, grandmothers are not supposed to be laser cooks. They are supposed to wear ample white aprons and bake gingerbread men. Somehow or other, the idea of my mother's "selling out" to the microwave industry really seemed a great disappointment.

In fact, I didn't even understand why anyone would *want* to roast a chicken in four-and-a-half minutes. You see, some of the most pleasant memories of my growing-up years revolve around lengthy discussions my mother and I had while "hanging around" the kitchen. I liked the kitchen. So I have never really understood why anyone would spend money to stay out of it. It seems to me that people eager to flee the kitchen are simply missing out on all the fun.

In my experience, our most important discussions happen in the kitchen. Not in the living room. In the living room, most of us tend to sit and be convivial together. We chat, we banter, we discuss the latest books, and we answer questions about what we have been doing with ourselves lately. But in the kitchen, we pour our guts out.

The kitchen lends itself well to the discussion of important matters. First of all, it offers a captive audience in the form of the cook, who is sort of omnipresently simmering something or stirring something "until it thickens" (which can be forever).

Secondly, the kitchen smells good, and it is usually, by virtue of all four burners going, a warm place to be. For most of us, it is particularly pleasant to discuss important matters amid nice smells and warm air.

Finally, it is often much easier to share our most intimate feelings and heartaches if it *seems* like we are not actually doing it. If what we are doing is dicing the onions or peeling the potatoes — if we are somewhat diverted from the strength of our feelings for a moment — it seems somehow easier to express them. After all, if we become too embarrassed or overwrought, we can simply return to making the salad with a vengeance. So the kitchen is often an especially "safe" place to talk. No one is calling us on the carpet, as it were, to Open-Up-Your-Heart-And-Be-Quick-About-It.

Certainly, the creation of this low-key, cozy atmosphere is therapeutic for adults. But for children, I think it is crucial.

It's hard for a child to talk about how he might flunk gym or how the other kids made fun of him on the way home from school, if he is supposed to make an appointment to do it. Children, like all of us, are only human, and it is sometimes easier to amble around a pain before we finally tear the band-aid off and expose it to the healing air.

I remember doing that sort of ambling in the kitchen.

I would come home from school and see Mom in the kitchen simmering chili. I would open the refrigerator, close it, and say, "Why don't we ever have anything good to eat?"

Then I would go downstairs, take off my sweater, throw it on the floor, come upstairs, open the refrigerator door again, and say, "What's for dinner?" Mom would tell me. "Ugh," I would say. "We just had that."

Then I would call my best friend and be told that she was at a yearbook meeting. I would walk around the living room, pick up a magazine, throw it on the sofa, go into the kitchen again, and open the refrigerator. I would tell my mother that I did not *want* a nice, fresh apple. Then I would heave an enormous sigh, look in the cupboards, leave them open, listen to Mom ask if there was anything wrong, and tell her, "No." I would go downstairs, bang on the piano, have an argument with a sibling, come upstairs and look in the refrigerator, shut it again, and agree to chop the green peppers for Mom.

Then — observing her still simmering chili on the stove — I would sit down on a stool and say, "You know that stupid Tommy Morgan? I hate that stupid Tommy Morgan!"

Then Mom, not looking up from the chili (most moms knew you'd stop talking if they looked up from the chili) would say, "Oh, really? Why do you feel that way?" And somewhere between chopping the green peppers and running the dishwasher, I would tell her.

So I speak in praise of simmering. It deserves its own preservation fund, like the ones for whales and bald eagles. Microwave ovens may "free" us from the kitchen by taking all the time out of cooking. But they take all the love out of it, too.

As much as we would like to deny it, women are in truth discovering that children rarely need their mothers at their mothers' convenience. Those of us who have tried — and tried and tried and tried — to make the "quality time" theory work have, quite simply, come up empty-handed. A working mother from Virginia, whose current employer allows a seven-to-four workday so she can be home when her daughter returns from school, remembers a time circumstances weren't so favorable: "I would be tense during the entire drive home from work, thinking 'I must relate with Emma, I must relate with Emma.' But when I arrived home, Emma wouldn't want to relate. Emma would want to watch television."

A former working mother from Michigan remarks: "When I got home at night, I read to my son and played with him. I gave him lots of undivided attention. But you know, it wasn't 'quality time.' I think it's a myth to say you can give quality time to a child after eight hours of work. I was tired and washed out. Many nights we ate TV dinners because I was too tired to cook. Although I read to Danny and played with him, I forced myself to do it. In spite of how dearly I loved my son, I really didn't enjoy him. I was too tired."

## "Quality Time"
## An Empty Exercise for Mothers at Home, Too

Trying to make a success out of "quality time" has also disappointed many at-home mothers, for parenting "experts" have made them just as conscious of the importance of one-on-one interaction. It seems that no matter how thoughtfully we plan or present a special mother-child activity, it rarely equals the exultation of those uncapturable moments that seem to fall in and out of our hands like dandelion dust, without benefit of plan or appointment.

"I recall a moment one day [last] fall," writes Joanne Bruun of Ellicott City, Maryland. "It was a beautiful September morning, a day that offered the promise of fall but retained the fullness of summer. The sky was brilliant. The air was warm and held September's special stillness, yet the trees hung lush and ripe with not a leaf lost. My baby awoke from her nap and she was warm with sleep. I carried her downstairs and as I did, Billy Joel's "Leave a Tender Moment Alone" came on the radio. The song sang to me, the day spoke to me, and the baby warmed to me. I began to dance with her, just my little miracle and I dancing on a perfect fall day. One of the joys of being at home is being open to just such a moment."

But when we are at home full-time, we find ourselves open to other kinds of moments as well — the moments when we wonder if we are really doing right by our children; the times we wonder if someone else might not do a better job of raising our children than we could. In the following essay, Linda Burton considers these times.

# Unquality Time

## by Linda Burton

When I was twenty-two and gorgeous, I saw this woman in the parking lot at the supermarket. She was driving a large station wagon, and she was yelling loudly at three disheveled children who had fudgesicle dripping all over their faces and onto their clothes. Groceries were spilling out of bags onto the back seat and floor. The woman's hair was uncombed and her clothes looked as if she had slept in them. With complete disgust, I pointed her out to a friend. "Ugh," I said. "I will never let *that* happen to me!" This unhappy-looking woman in the station wagon represented everything I never wanted to be.

At the time, I remember discussing with my friend how this obviously miserable woman would be a lot happier in an office. Her children drove her crazy, I suspected, and what she needed was a lot more mental stimulation. What her children needed, I thought, was a calm, loving mother. There was no question in my mind that she should "get a job and leave her kids with a sitter or something."

I forgot the incident until quite recently while in the car (a station wagon, as it happens) with my own children. I had had a sleepless night, dealing with the latest in the progression of flus and viruses which seem to adopt my children whenever the temperature dips below fifty-two degrees, and I was not in a good mood. In my rush to get out and pick up a new prescription at the drugstore, I had thrown on some soiled khakis and a T-shirt and had ignored my hair entirely, hoping I could just "shake" it into shape along the way. My thoughts were focused on the approaching evening.

Several months earlier, I had agreed to teach a few one-night classes for the county's Continuing Education Department. It seemed like a smart move. I thought teaching these classes would be a good way to keep up my professional resume — put on "hold" for the years I was raising my family — and get me out in the world of adult stimulation. Best of all, the classes carried the extra bonus of requiring only a very small investment of my time. The day of the first class had arrived. Despite considerable advance notice, I was still not completely prepared. As I stuffed my overcoated children into their carseats, fussing with securing the various latches and locks, my mind was racing furiously ahead, mentally trying to tie up the loose ends of my class outline. Why did I ever agree to teach these classes?

Fear gripped me for a minute as I pictured myself standing dumbstruck in front of twenty-eight students, without the dimmest notion of how to begin. These thoughts consumed all my attention as I wearily came to a stop at the traffic light signaling the edge of our community. Just at this moment, the eighteen-month-old decided to throw his bottle on the floor, jarring the top loose and allowing apple juice to flood the floor and creep under the passenger seat. He screamed loudly for me to pick up the bottle. My three-year-old began to whine at a grating decibel level, and his brother screamed louder. The light turned green.

Angrily, I jerked the car over to the side of the road and lit into both children in a very unpleasant way. I had had it. My nerves were raw, my mind was flaccid from being pulled in spokelike directions; I looked terrible. I wasn't prepared for my class that evening. And at that moment, it felt like my predicament was all their fault. For what must have been a full minute, I screamed uncontrollable vituperation at my children. As I slumped against the car seat in exhaustion, I noticed that the traffic light had turned red again, and there was a girl — about twenty-two — in an MG directly opposite me. Beautifully dressed and looking terrific, she was staring at the picture I presented in horror and disgust. Our eyes met only for an instant before the light turned again and she went on her way, but it was a moment of complete insight.

I had become the woman I never wanted to be. I was the living caricature of everything that could go wrong with motherhood. I felt like there was only one place to turn. If being a mother was this exhausting, this draining — if it meant that my frustrations would make me turn on my children so cruelly — then I should go back to work. The mounting tensions in my life had caused me to be grossly unjust to my children, and nothing was worth that. Knowing that I had frightened them in the bargain made me feel even worse.

Maybe it would be better, I thought, if I were to go to work and hand my children over to someone kinder than I was, someone who was "better" with children than I was. Surely there were people who were "made" for the job of mothering; it's just that I wasn't one of them. Perhaps if I were away from my children for much of the day, I would appreciate them more at day's end. I wanted to feel good about myself as a mother, and it seemed at that moment as if the only way I was going to feel good was to turn over most of the job to somebody else.

But for the time being, the three of us were stuck together in a very small space, and we couldn't really walk away from the problem. Somehow, I had to disentangle us all from the frenzy of the last several minutes.

I apologized.

It was not easy, because I was feeling as victimized as they were.

"Look guys," I said. "I'm really sorry I yelled at you. It wasn't right. I wasn't fair to you. I shouldn't have done it. Do you know why I was yelling?"

The three-year-old solemnly nodded his head. "You were mad," he said.

"Honey," I explained, "I wasn't mad at you."

"Then who were you mad at?"

"I don't think I was really mad at all; I was tired, and sometimes just being tired makes you feel mad. Isn't that silly?" He didn't say anything. "But you know what else, honey?" I added. "There's something I have to do that's kind of scaring me, and that made me act mad. Sometimes we act mad when really what we are is scared." He seemed to absorb the complex logic easier than I would have thought. "Did I scare you, honey?" I asked. He nodded. "I'll bet I did," I said.

We discussed it a bit longer and we all seemed to feel much better as we continued our drive to the store.

At that unlikely moment, I made the firm decision to remain at home with my children. I knew no one could have taught them as much as I did in that car. I also knew that there was no job that could teach me as much as I had learned from them during that one incident.

What had they learned? First of all, they learned that it is okay to be mad. If my children saw me only during my "good" times and not during my bad, how might they feel about themselves when *they* got mad? Second, they learned that when we don't do the right thing, there is usually something that can be done about it. We do not allow ourselves to continue repeating an unkind behavior. Finally, they learned that sometimes when we feel angry, something else may really be going on, such as fear or lack of sleep. I hope this episode taught my children to occasionally look beneath their own anger to see what else might really be bothering them.

From this very bad time — this supremely "unquality" time — I learned why it is crucial for me to be at home with my children.

---

About Our Children

My purpose in being with them was to teach them how to live successfully, how to get through the vicissitudes of life as well and as happily as possible. I suddenly realized that I could not possibly teach them those important lessons if they did not see me go through some dismal times. I knew that my children would be carefully examining how I handled my own problems to use as a model for overcoming their own.

So much of our success in life, after all, is measured by how well we are able to get through the times that aren't so good — the times when we are too tired; when we're frightened; when we fail. If we are not around to serve as examples for our children for how to get through those times and emerge victorious, then how will they learn the lessons?

Few of us, I learned, are really "born" for the job of mothering. Rather, being a good mother is a privilege earned through hard work and a continual, daily recommitment to the importance of that work. It means being willing enough to confront the very worst in ourselves, and brave enough not to run away from it when the going gets rough. In point of fact, mothering is rough and scary work. I understand fully how great the temptation is to hand the job over to somebody else — somebody "born" to do it.

Since that day at the stoplight, I have wanted to quit with great regularity. But then I have never begun a new job that I didn't periodically want to quit — especially when I was afraid that I was not going to do well. I would come home and say, "This job isn't for me; I'm no good at it. I'll never learn to do it." A real terror at the idea of failure has always made the idea of "giving up the ship" especially attractive to me. Unfortunately, however, whenever I have chosen to "give up the ship," I have also chosen never to experience the sea.

It seems to me that when we feel our most inadequate, we are presented with our greatest opportunity for self-revelation and growth. We are presented with an opportunity to take a chance on ourselves and come out on top — to build a confidence-reinforcing chain of success. So I do not, at bottom, believe that mothers are either "born" for the job or not. We may be frightened of mothering. We may not feel up to it, we may run from its challenges, and we may call our fear a simple inborn ineptitude for the job. But then we will never experience the sea, and we will never see the view from the mountaintop.

## Children Gain Real Independence by Learning
## To Be on Their Own— Not Having To Be on Their Own

One of the greatest joys of motherhood is watching our children become independent of us. To share in those moments when a child first begins to realize that he might amount to something in this world, to urge him to try his wings more and more, and to applaud his victories as he becomes an independent, self-confident little human are among the most gloriously satisfying experiences a mother can have.

But there are different ways to teach a child to become independent. Someone can take us to a swimming pool when we are small, throw us in the water and shout, "SWIM!" Or they can gently bounce us in the water when we are babies, play with us in the water when we're a little bigger, and then, eventually, teach us how to float, do the crawl, sidestroke, backstroke, and breaststroke, and then say, "SWIM!"

Doubtless either method would produce an adept swimmer — and a child taught by the first may indeed become an independent swimmer long before the second. But to what avail?

If a mother simply wanted her children to learn independence, she could look out for them much less, spend less time with them, think about them less. But most mothers want their children to learn more than that. It is the quality of a child's independence that concerns most mothers: Was it born of necessity or of self-confidence? Do their children know they can make it on their own because they are rich in resources? Or do they know they can make it on their own because, by golly, they had to? Can they help other people along the way because somebody took the time to help them? Or do they ignore the needs of other people because no one was there when they had a need? Will they be able to combat any potential challenges to their independence because they feel nurtured, secure in themselves and their abilities? Or will they be able to combat any potential challenges to their independence because they had to fight to get it, and they'll fight to keep it?

In their quiet moments of reckoning — of measuring humanity against detached textbooks, and intuition against edict — most mothers come to terms with what they truly believe is best for their children.

# There Is No Specific Age
# When a Child Stops Needing You

It is ironic that a nation that has developed a veritable fetish of "bonding" with an infant at birth advises us of the wisdom of leaving them as early as a tender six weeks of age. As child care "experts" conduct studies and draft papers and haggle over pinpointing the time at which a child no longer needs our full-time attention, mothers themselves have long known the answer.

Mary Molegraaf, a mother of three school-age children from Grandville, Michigan, observes, "I was so anxious for this time to come so that I could get out of the house and go to work. Now that it's here, I feel that it's more important than ever for me to be home to get [the children] off to school in the morning and be here when they get home."

Kathleen Reed, a mother of teens in Hagerstown, Maryland, experienced this feeling more than once:

"When my kids were toddlers, I thought I'd go to work when they got in school. But then there was the problem of what to do when they're sick, school is called off, summer vacations, and so on. So then I said, 'When they get to middle school.'

"Granted, I do have more time now for myself, and they could cope if I weren't here. But yesterday was a perfect example of why I'm glad I'm around when they need me. It was the first day of the new marking period at school. They both came home with a list of things they needed 'right away.'

"We jumped in the car and went shopping for these items, then rushed home, and while I fixed dinner, they did homework — in the kitchen so I could explain things. We had to leave right after eating because my son had a basketball game. I didn't have to fret about the dishes or what to wear to work or the laundry. I could go and enjoy his game.

"He is not the greatest basketball player, but he made one key play. Then, he looked over and grinned at me. I wouldn't want anyone else to have that smile. To me, it meant just as much as his first step, or his first tooth. These are my rewards."

Dee Cosola of Leona Valley, California, did go back to work briefly. "I am forty-seven and have three grown children, all married and doing fine. I was home with them until the youngest was sixteen; then I listened to the world and sought a career so I could be *fulfilled*.

My sixteen-year-old daughter became very depressed and I knew something was wrong. She needed me as much at sixteen years as she did at sixteen months."

"Sure we have outgrown the 'first tooth' and 'first steps,'" says Donna Harper of St. Louis, Missouri, "but somehow Rob's grand slam home run, or Tim's 'most valuable player' in the holiday soccer tournament can be just as great an accomplishment, and I'm lucky to be home to share it. My girls are grown, one at college and one on the way, but they have their needs, too. Whether it's a sympathetic ear to steer Missy through 'puppy love,' or listening to the long-distance tears when Christa decides to be 'strung out' about her exams, I'm still glad to be here for them."

◆　　◆　　◆

Not many of us realized, when we first set out on this obscure road, the impact children would have on our lives. Yet for all the uncertainty, and the sometimes frightening challenges we see on the horizon, most of us still find ourselves surprisingly eager to complete the journey.

*Chapter 4*

# Startling Realizations
# and Gentle Discoveries...
# ... About Our Work

**A**lmost any mother will confess that the time she knew the most about raising children and running a home was before she had either one. In those privileged days of unconstrained, child-free living, most of us knew exactly how *our* children would behave, and exactly how *our* homes would function. We also knew precisely where our mothers and friends had gone wrong, and how to avoid their mistakes.

Not long after the birth of our first child, many of us were knocking at the doors of those same friends to ask advice. It wasn't quite as easy as we thought to plan a week's worth of menus or to produce an infant who slept through the night. And it looked as if life might be getting more, not less, complicated.

Wanting to stay at home with our children, and being good at it, are two very different things. In this age when women are not encouraged to learn anything about mothering or managing a home until they are in fact mothering and managing a home, it is easy to feel inadequate. Whether we have been home since our wedding day or whether we suddenly leave a long and successful career, we are likely to be struggling with many of the same obstacles — and many of the same feelings.

## The Transition from Expectations to Realities

Perhaps the most basic feeling shared by those who stay home is the shock of discovering that life at home isn't what we expected. "Before my first child came along," writes Donna Garver Henry of Lawrenceville, New Jersey, "I had believed that mothering was one continuous love affair between baby and parents. I had envisioned a pretty woman in a flowing chiffon dress running through a field of daisies with a cherry-cheeked cherub toddling after her." Donna found the reality of a newborn quite different. She continues, "Motherhood had been so idealized that I was totally unprepared for its practical application. Nothing had prepared me for the anger I felt after all my efforts to quiet my fussy child had failed."

Ann Folker Antrim of Eureka, California, who came home to care for her baby after a seven-year career as an English teacher, describes the difference between what she expected and what she found:

"While I had worked, I'd idealized the wonderful, freedom-filled lives of housewives. I envied the possible spontaneity in their lives. I

---

*After hearing "Focus on the Family"'s program with you involved, it helped me make some major decisions in my life. I am a wife and a mother of a fine Christian husband and a sixteen-year-old son and a thirteen-year-old daughter. I had been trying to be "superwoman" for ten years. And recently my physical and emotional health was beginning to suffer. The stress level that I functioned under was robbing me of all that was precious to me—namely, time with my family.*

*Your program gave me the courage I needed to approach my husband about drastically changing our lifestyle. Much to my surprise and joy, he was 100% supportive of my every suggestion! My cessation from the work force has meant a lot of changes for us — all positive. We sold both of our expensive cars and purchased a new but practical station wagon; we are now tithing for the first time ever; we are living within a carefully planned but comfortable budget; we are spending an exponentially increased amount of time together with each other — as a couple, as a family, as parent-child; so many of the "I wish I had time for . . ." things are being accomplished; there is relaxation and fun and laughter in our home. We had bought the inflated ideal of acquiring "things" instead of memories.*

*A recent poll of my children and my husband showed a unanimous bias to* never, *never go back to our old way of life where I was gone until 6:00 P.M. nightly, brought home work at night, did work on weekends, and was always irritated and stressed.*

*As our children grow and leave our home and we grow old together as a couple, I will be forever grateful to your broadcast and how God used it to change our lives.*

*Donna Kleinert, Austin, Texas*

---

imagined being able to drink in each season by taking long walks —
a luxury I didn't have working inside, Monday through Friday, fall
through spring. I dreamed about all the projects I would get done and
new talents I would develop.

"And then . . . the baby arrived. I lived on the baby's time. He slept;
I slept. He ate; I got thirsty. He cried in the middle of the night; I got
up to comfort him. When he was asleep, I missed him. Sometimes
when he was awake, I wished he'd fall asleep so I could get things
done. Every so often, I'd realize a week had passed since my last quiet
thinking time."

Celia Leftwich Denning, of Salem, Virginia, pictured coming home
after five years as a working mother would mean "warm breakfasts,
my daughter arriving home from kindergarten in her yellow rain
slicker for a Campbell's-soup-commercial-style lunch, and doing
laundry on Wednesday." Michele Pauly, of Melbourne, Florida, who
worked full-time as a bank officer until her oldest child was four
years old, recalls, "I thought I would have time for making bread,
sewing, painting, volunteering, exercise class, two or three classes at
college, not to mention all the fun activities I planned to do with my
children."

Like others before them, these women found "home" was not quite
what they had envisioned. Reports Michele: "What a shock to find
out I not only didn't have time for all these activities; I barely got done
the same things I did when I worked! I felt so disorganized, ineffi-

---

*I grew up in an urban area of Queens, New York. From there I proceeded onto
schooling and a career in Manhattan. Eight years ago, my husband and I took on
the "American Dream" and moved into the suburbs to open a business and start a
family.*

*My first child is six years old now but when she was two I found a deep
unsettling taking place within me. I thought motherhood was going to be the end-
all of my life, yet the loneliness and loss of my former identity hit hard. I searched
out information and found The Mother Center of Suffolk. This is a place where
mothers meet with mothers to discuss themselves and the many roles women are
faced with in today's changing society. I found a true sense of myself in the
meetings.*

*There are still moments since I've had my second child when I feel isolated and
motherhood is overwhelming, but I [now] have the center to turn to. Then I see all
the wonderful aspects of motherhood; and being home for my family and myself
takes on more meaning.*

*Karen D'Onofrio, Holbrook, Long Island, New York*

---

cient, and frustrated." Though there were pleasant surprises as well, each of these mothers went through a period of transition that required surviving some pretty dejecting and uncertain moments.

## The Question of a New Identity

When we first discover that the realities of life at home contradict the idealized vision we once entertained, we are often thrown into an unanticipated search for who we really are. Suddenly the picture of what we thought we would be like as a mother and wife disappears, and we aren't sure where to go for a replacement. We wonder if all mothers at home trip over the same stumbling blocks or if we alone are ignorant of the secrets of getting better organized, dealing patiently with children, and keeping a house magazine-perfect.

We ponder . . . if a mother at home doesn't do what we thought she did, what does she do? And, either subconsciously or with studious diligence, we begin to examine all that our new role as mother and wife at home might include. Like a toddler on a quest for new limits in a recently expanded world, we test the waters of various aspects of our chosen work. We may throw ourselves into cleaning until we recognize that it consumes us, or concentrate day and night on decorating until we fear it is done at the expense of more important efforts. In reaction, we might switch to hovering over our children's lives as we attempt to figure out where to draw the line between helping and hindering growth.

---

*I am a fifty-five year old widow who was always at home. There was nothing and no one more important than my husband and daughter. My husband was a sergeant in the Air Force for over twenty years and at that time there was very little money, but the coffers of happiness were overflowing.*

*I always felt as though God placed those two wonderful human beings in my care and I cared more than I can explain, and I'm so glad that I did, because I lost my husband when he was fifty-two years old with cancer. Soon after his death, I became ill with a chronic disease. I still have very little money, but I am left with a wonderful caring daughter, who, by the way, is also a mother at home, and I have no guilt and no regrets.*

*The two years before my husband's death, we talked constantly and he said the kindest words about things I did for him that at the time were such small things, but evidently to him were very important.*

*There are times when I look back and ponder whether or not I should have taken another route, yet deep down in my inner self I know I would do it the same way. It was a happy, delightful journey.*

*Jane DeBusschere, Oshkosh, Wisconsin*

About Our Work

Since each victory through trial-and-error provides only a clue to the mother at home we now want to be, the search continues. We try reading books by "experts" and imitating neighbors who seem to "do it right." We experiment with labor-saving gadgets, time-saving schedules, and space-saving devices. Sometimes we try doing everything in balance and to perfection, and other times we simply try ignoring our responsibilities, in the hope that no one will care.

And every day we fit another piece into our jigsaw puzzle picture of what it means to be at home with children — at least in our particular time, in our particular neighborhood, in our particular family.

## Children Set the Boundaries of Our Days

As we experiment with the endless list of activities that could consume our time, we happen upon occasional discoveries — nuggets of wisdom that help us select one thing over another and aid us in giving shape to our open-ended days. We learn quickly that in the business of staying home with children, children regulate the events of the hours — and children can be completely unpredictable. As Michele Pauly explains:

"Although I spent time with my daughter when I worked, it wasn't necessarily 'on demand' time. I had certain things that needed to be

---

*Twenty-seven or so years ago, we founded a little organization called La Leche League, begun to help mothers who wanted to nurse their babies. Over the years, it has grown in response, I am convinced, to the very real and urgent desire on the part of mothers to do what they instinctively believed was the right thing to do. Part and parcel of all this, of course, was the concept of what we call "full-time mothering."*

*Having raised our family with the conviction that staying at home and being a full-time wife and mother is the right and best way to fulfill the promises of marriage, I can look back and be thankful that I was able to do just that. My children feel the same way, and of our eleven, five are now married, all with full-time, stay-at-home "keepers of the home." (I'm still going at it, as our youngest is just thirteen.)*

*Being a founding mom of La Leche League, I can say that doing the job right entails a great deal more than just nursing a baby... it's more than just full-time mothering, it's recognizing what marriage is all about and trying to live up to it, "for better, for worse," and all that good stuff.*

*Mary White, River Forest, Illinois*

---

done each evening and weekend; therefore, I planned specific activities for her to keep her from 'underfoot.'

"Now I am accessible at any time. When I worked, someone else kissed all the hurts away. Someone else rocked her to sleep. Someone else fed her, changed her, played with her, and answered the millions of questions. Someone else spent 'on demand' time with her.

"'On demand' time takes a lot of time!! Especially now that I have two children, I know why all those activities don't get done on the time schedule I had planned. They do get done — but more on the schedule that my children set. And you know, it doesn't even matter."

The longer we are at home, the more we realize why it is so difficult for anyone but a mother to measure or define the work she does, and sometimes the definition is even beyond her. In a sense, her real work is NOT those activities others can most easily quantify — the housecleaning, the cooking, the driving, the shopping. Her real work is handling the interruptions that punctuate her day, the exchanges — brief or extended, simple or profound — with her children. As Pat Cundick, a time management specialist and mother of five who lives in the Northwest, points out, "If housework and a child's needs clash, which is the interruption?"

In the following essay, Linda Burton examines the true nature of a mother's day, and answers a commonly asked question.

---

*At a time when I was so tired of hearing, "What do you do?" — my reply, "I'm at home raising my children," and then, "Is that all?" or "Why don't you work?" — it was so refreshing to hear from other mothers that what we're doing is worth it!! I find the biggest problem with being at home is the lack of recognition and value placed on what I do. It took the longest time to adjust to very few "pats-on-the-back." I had been used to working where every week there was the paycheck, a raise, promotion, etc. When my daughter was born, I stopped work and suddenly all praise stopped, too. In fact, I was constantly defending my choice to stay at home!*

*For me, it has been a great choice to stay at home — the work is hard but the love from my family is wonderful!*

*Janis D. Malone, Clinton, Connecticut*

About Our Work

# What Do You Do All Day?

## by Linda Burton

"What do you do all day?" a single friend of mine asked recently. "Do you really do anything at home?"

I stared at her blankly for a moment. I do so much at home, I had absolutely no idea where to begin. Apparently assuming that my temporary silence meant I had nothing to say, my friend continued forthrightly on. "Don't you feel," she suggested, lowering her voice to the chummy, conspiratorial level of a first-year sorority sister, "that your mind is too good to be at home?"

"Too good to be at home?" I wondered. On the contrary. I thought my mind was too good *not* to be at home. The problem seems to be explaining this to other people. And it's not that I haven't had friends who were willing to listen. I have. I even had one single friend who volunteered to follow me around or to replace me entirely for one day, to try to discover for herself the intellectual demands and satisfactions of being another person's full-time mother. But she wouldn't have understood.

From the outside, a mother's life looks very different than it feels from the inside. That is why most of the studies about what mothers actually do with their time all day are almost always inaccurate. From the outside, our lives may well appear to be fragmented and frustrating. The structure of what we do looks menial and repetitive. And throughout a typical day, we are called upon to change directions as often as a squirrel trying to cross an interstate highway. The view from the inside, however, is rife with excitement and surprises. From the inside, many mothers see themselves regularly searching the depths of their brains and the perimeters of their educations, looking for answers they are not even sure are there.

The fact is that another human being can rarely understand the nature of a mother's work because her job can only be understood in terms of cumulative experience, and every day is completely different. To people on the outside, the work that a mother does — the guiding, teaching, hounding, and entreating — is loud, repetitious, and often seemingly fruitless. Our efforts seem to take forever. Our rewards, though enormous, appear to come and go in an instant. And more often than not, they are camouflaged as a rather simple part of a thoroughly ordinary day.

How could I explain to a casual observer, for instance, what was really going on while I watched my son run down a steep hill and run exultantly back to the top? How can I recapture just what it was like, watching him slowly overcome his initial fear? How long would another person sit and listen to me recount each experience with that hill — how at first, he wouldn't even go to the edge; then he'd go down a little bit and run back, then down a little more . . . Who's going to sit and listen to that?

But I shared a moment when a human being conquered a fear and felt his first exhilarating taste of accomplishment — the moment when he first began to realize that he might do something in the world. So often, our achievements have a history, to which only we are privy. To understand the real nature of full-time mothering, it's like the old rejoinder to a misunderstood joke: "You had to be there."

I am at home to help influence and shape the lives of my children, in a way that I hope will create the greatest happiness for them and for the people around them. What I *do* with my days, toward this end, is to teach hundreds of ten-second lessons which explore every area of human knowledge and experience. At home I don't just use my education; I run out of it, and have to hustle off to the library for more. I know this for a fact. My children certainly benefit from it. But again, how do I explain this to other people?

It is easy to see a mother teaching her child his ABC's, or working with him on how to tie his shoelaces, and make a little note that the mother spent "X" amount of time teaching her child a skill. But how about the much less tangible, and even more important, teaching that we do? How about the teaching that a statistician, efficiency expert, or sociologist really cannot notate or classify because it is invisible to the naked eye? A lot of people can teach my children skills. I, on the other hand, teach them that they are loved; that they can function as independent, self-confident little people; that they are capable of great things; and that when I say I'm "looking out for 'Number One,'" I mean I'm looking out for them.

I wonder how an observing social scientist would manage to catalogue the time I spend all day working near my children. I figure he would be able to mark down the negligible-to-nonexistent amount of time I spend playing with my children with no trouble. That time is easy to quantify and isolate. But I am entirely certain that that time has nowhere near the same impact on my children than does their daily, rather pedestrian observance of how I act and what I do day in and day out. How would an outside observer manage to quantify the amount of time in which I serve as a living, breathing, consistent example to my children of how to do everything from answering the doorbell to mediating major conflicts?

Children who only play in the general vicinity of their mothers are picking up lessons from her, with nary the exchange of a word. How does Mommy treat other people? What makes her curious or excited? What if Mommy wants to learn something new — where does she go to learn it? What kind of music does Mommy like — does it make her happy or sad or want to dance? How does Mommy talk? What language does she use? Does Mommy share? Why does Mommy like books so much — is there something really good inside of books?

As mothers at home, we are "interacting" with our children, in one form or another, twenty-four hours a day. Often, even we do not realize how much we are interacting or how much of a real effect our presence has on our children until we see them begin to imitate the behavior or espouse the values of someone else, in whose care we have left them.

Only recently, I was taking my children along with me to the grocery store — an activity which many an outside observer would have labeled "mindless carpooling" to perform the "menial task" of getting the family groceries. Without a Child Guidance puzzle or a Playskool building block in sight, and with no other visible or obvious activity between us, my children and I managed to enrich each other's lives considerably during that time.

We discussed what we saw on the drive, what it meant, where we were going, what we were doing that evening, and what we thought about it all. We talked about why some helicopters flew in formation, we pointed out Queen Anne's Lace and talked about where it grew and how to preserve it if we wanted to. We discussed what a "staple" was (the kind you get at the grocery store and the kind you use on papers) and how that was different from a "stable" which led to an animated conversation about the little baby Jesus and why he was born and how we might find out what myrrh looked like. In the store, we talked endlessly (it seemed) about what vitamins were in what foods and what the potassium in bananas did for our bodies and why they were better than Fruit Loops. We addressed a variety of economic issues, as well as why we read food labels, how to read food labels, why you don't push in line, and why they tell us some things on television commercials that are not true.

◆
◆
◆
◆
◆
◆

Needless to say, there are many people who would have observed me with my children that day and concluded that "she only took them to the grocery store." And yet, believe me, it is not the thirty minutes of intensive playtime or lesson time with Mommy that is going to shape our children's lives, so much as the day in and day out view from the front seat of the grocery cart.

## A Mother's Job is Making Memories

Once, in a classroom of young mothers who were discussing the hardships of the preschool years, a mother of two commented: "One day when I had just had it, I called my mother. I asked her, 'How did you ever do this without going crazy? The kids are whiny, I can hardly get a meal on the table, I clean house all day long and the next day I face the same mess all over again.' She told me I had the wrong perspective on my job, that a mother wasn't just a babysitter, cook, and housekeeper. She told me a mother's job is to make memories."

As we each begin to clarify which activities ought to have priority on a day-to-day basis in our lives, we come to realize that whether we spend long hours reading to children or creating savory meals or perfecting the kitchen decor, we are contributing to the concept our children will have of "home." We are stockpiling memories for them to use in the years ahead. We are filling the corners of their minds with sights and sounds and smells that will re-emerge just when they need to remember that somewhere they are loved, whether they falter or whether they flourish.

Linda Burton contemplates the challenges of providing those kinds of memories in today's society.

# Looking for Home

## by Linda Burton

I want to move to the country, on most days. And when my husband lets me know that the country isn't available because of its commuting distance from his office, then I yearn for another century. If only I could have lived in another era, some tea and croquet, slowish kind of time, when I could have spent the morning hours putting up preserves from the strawberries my children had picked in the garden out back. Instead, I spend the morning filling up my car at the self-serve gas island, so I can drive four miles to a seventeen-aisle-wide supermarket to pick up some commercial preserves full of additives, food coloring, and too much sugar. Is this any way to live?

Like an awful lot of Americans today, I am growing as concerned with the quality of my life as I am with the speed of its passing. And the advertising industry knows it. For while article after article still appears in magazines extolling the pleasures of stress and saluting ambitious, hard-driven, "Type-A" lifestyles, it is the advertisers who are paid to know already what many of us are just beginning to figure out: that what we are really in the market for these days is an afternoon sitting around with Grandpa, sipping lemonade and swatting flies on the front porch.

In so many places, I see a real yearning for greater stability and more time in our lives, for a sense of grace and permanence and continuity instead of a mere collage of almost unrelated fragments, thrown together at top speed. The sad thing is that we are trying to buy what really cannot be bought; and that so many people are trying to sell it to us, anyway.

Almost daily, another new product appears on the marketplace which is advertised to suggest a slowed-down lifestyle, a leisurely morning having coffee with a friend, or mixing up a cherry drink in a frosty pitcher so the neighborhood kids can fill their thirst and get back to their baseball game. The fact that our friends are often away from home when we call for coffee, and that part of the neighborhood baseball team may well be down at the school in the extended-care program does not alter our attraction to the product that suggests they are not.

Each of the products featuring this slowed-down lifestyle has an advertising company behind it that is working hard to capitalize on the feelings so many of us are missing. In the midst of our frenetic, over-extended days, anything which implies a sense of tranquility, simplicity, and infinite time has an almost unbeatable appeal. And we are led to believe that we can buy into this more appealing life if only we choose the right product.

In the housing market, for instance, we have begun to beg for Victorian-style homes, and for the reinstitution of the old-fashioned front porch. The reason, I think, is because homes like these evoke images of long, lazy evening hours exclaiming at the fireflies, enjoying the children, and chatting with the passing neighbors. But even though we adorn our porches with the requisite wicker furniture, potted ferns, and wrought-iron bird cages from years past, I drive through communities full of porches like these that nobody ever sits on.

The rise in popularity of "country" magazines, as well as country decorating styles, is another indication, I think, of our effort to reach out and reclaim the simple, gentle experience of our own day-to-day lives — the feeling that we are really living them, instead of only administering them. The components of these decorating styles — the plain, homey, nurturing feelings elicited by the quilts, wooden ducks, and stenciled walls of "the country look" — or the cozy, nest-like feelings projected by the accumulated memorabilia, overstuffed furniture, and the lavish creature comforts common to the English variation on the same theme, all seem designed to put their decorative arms around us and invite us to settle back and relax.

Wouldn't it be nice, we imagine, to spend a little time savoring where we are, instead of worrying over whether we're going to be on time for wherever we are supposed to be next? Yet for some reason, this longed-for reality always seems to be just about as elusive as "one day soon," or "only an hour out of town." In the meantime, we settle for samples.

We buy bread reminiscent of turn-of-the-century home-town bakeries, where the owner knew our name and kept a loaf of our favorite seeded-rye under the wooden counter for us. We select the cookies which appear the most "homemade." Yet cookies that were made at home are valued for the experience of making them as much as they are the pleasure of eating them. How can we replace that familiar hour or two spent with our children, as they insist on tasting the dry ingredients and vie with each other for the best view of the proceedings and the fullest beater? Although we cannot toss those few agreeable hours into our shopping carts, I am convinced that the experience is really what we want to buy.

And we are beginning to make celebrities out of people who celebrate the ordinary.

National magazine columnist, Dee Hardie, has won over an enormous following of readers — not by relating the juicy vicissitudes of her harrowing climb up the corporate ladder — but simply by sharing her unaffected "View From Thornhill Farm." A wife, mother, and now grandmother, Mrs. Hardie writes about the commonplace events in her life: having tea and animal cookies with her grandchildren; detailing the best way to "pot" narcissus for spicy enjoyment over the Christmas season; conquering an old fear by joining the small, morning swimming class at the YWCA. Mrs. Hardie's fans, many of them victims of Fast Lane Fatigue, occasionally follow her as far as her front door, to see if they might be allowed to catch a wistful glimpse, however brief, of the life she chronicles.

Is it any wonder that we clamor for the revival of "oldie" TV shows like *The Andy Griffith Show* and *Leave It To Beaver*? Or that we occasionally gather around the radio to await the "News From Lake Wobegon"? Whether we're watching life go by from a chair in front of Floyd's Barber Shop in Mayberry, U.S.A., or ambling along with Garrison Keillor from the Chatterbox Cafe to the Pretty Good Grocery, most of us are there because we're tired of taking shortcuts. We're tired of catapulting ourselves through life, tired of cutting corners, tired of trying to keep too many balls in the air at the same time.

When we travel, we eschew the conveniences of the big chain motels and interstate highways in favor of staying at small bed-and-breakfast establishments on out-of-the-way back roads. And who could blame us? We are beginning to realize that when we rush along at seventy-five miles an hour in life, caught in the undercurrent of our own demanding schedules, we may be leaving much of what was ever really important to us trampled in our wake.

I remember one afternoon my older son and I ate our lunch while sitting on the front stoop of our townhouse, just absently kicking around a leaf or two with our toes and watching the squirrels shake acorns from the trees. Oh, we didn't discuss the mysteries of life or even raise any very profound questions. We just sort of "hung out" and were quiet together, exchanging occasional conversation and sharing a sandwich. But when I go back in my mind over the last five years to pick out the best times, the greatest times, I would certainly count that hour among them. And I have noticed that when my days begin to become over-scheduled, my son will wistfully request "lunch on the stoop" over the fancier noontime possibilities.

No matter what it is that ultimately brings our real priorities into sharp focus, most of us must at some point come to terms with the fact that we are not on this earth forever. And there is nothing so compelling as the awareness of our own mortality to bring what is truly important into immediate perspective. I remember reading once that when Nat King Cole discovered he was about to die, he remarked how odd it was that everything he used to think was important really didn't mean much to him, and how many of the things he used to brush aside as trivial, were all that really mattered in the world. I think of him sometimes, when I drive through communities full of empty porches. And I sometimes imagine him sitting on one of them, just taking in the breeze and chuckling over the darndest thing he has just read in the book on his lap. He always takes the time to give me a friendly wave, as I speed past.

When we begin to appraise our daily tasks according to new perspectives, such as the quality of the memories we're building, we also begin to shift our priorities. We see that we have a measure of control over what we sow for our children to reap in years ahead. For some of us, keeping an immaculate house, for instance, proves to be too time-consuming if we are to accomplish other goals as well. A father from Connecticut writes: "By choice, my wife works and I stay home and care for our two-year-old daughter. If you had asked me when I was a high school English teacher, I would not have believed how much energy and creativity it takes to take care of a home. [Several years ago] I visited a friend, a former colleague, who at the time had a young child. Toys littered the living room floor; the kitchen was awash with pots and pans. I ignorantly thought she was a sloppy housekeeper. Now that we have our own child, and I am home all day, my outlook has changed." Lynn Viale, of Gilroy, California states, "I want my eulogy to read more than: 'She was one great housekeeper.'"

While we may at first have emphasized keeping up the laundry, planning and preparing nutritious meals, and keeping the house in order, we soon realize how absolute is the transience of these years. We will always have meals to cook and clothes to clean, whether or not children scamper from room to room. But only now do we have the chance to make memories that will last a lifetime. From Beaver, Pennsylvania, Susan Koshute shares memories of her mother's efforts:

"Taking care of twelve children meant that most of her day was spent performing routine household tasks, but Mom also made time to plan special celebrations for ordinary days, holidays, and birthdays. She encouraged us to develop hobbies and showed appreciation for our elementary artwork by displaying it throughout the house.

"By generously sharing her time and talents with family, friends, and strangers, we were exposed to an invaluable philosophy of charity and goodwill that most of us children have adopted.

"I know that many of these memories didn't just happen; Mom planned them. She has often said what a wonderful career she chose by raising a family. My choice to be a full-time mother is a tribute to [my mother] and her efforts. And, already I have many happy memories of my own."

In the following essay, Linda Burton comments on the orchestration of such memories.

---

*I am an only child who wanted many children. I stayed at home to enjoy raising five, each now a responsible adult. I always felt so blessed to be able to be a homemaker rather than return to the business world. I was active in every facet of the family's life — i.e., organizations and teaching them to sew, bake bread and garden. My husband taught the boys woodworking. No, we were not a family of farmers, in fact, my husband traveled over the nation, home only on weekends much of the time, but the short time he was at home he was a loving father.*

*I want you to know there are many who remember a good life that seems to have gone out of style.*

*Beverly P. Taylor, Washington, Ohio*

# The Making of a Home

## by Linda Burton

My tenth grade English teacher, Miss Andrews, used to look forward to picture-taking day more than any other day in the school year. On that day, she said, all her students were at their best. It wasn't just that we all looked especially nice — we were expected to look that way on picture-taking day. It was that our behavior was so remarkable and our academic performance so exceptional. "When you get your bodies dressed up," said Miss Andrews, "the rest of you seems to get dressed up, too."

In many ways, it was Miss Andrews' picture-day principle that was to help shape my feelings about homemaking and its importance as a profession.

I began to notice, for instance, that when our table was nicely set, when fresh flowers were out, pillows fluffed, and wonderful smells were wafting from the kitchen, everyone's voice level would sink to half and people who ordinarily only argued together would make a special extra effort to be sensitive and conciliatory. When my immediate environment comforted me and responded to my individual needs — when it was "dressed up" — I was able to function at my very best. I began to see that good feelings did not necessarily "just happen" all the time, but that they often seemed to be, in some measure, designed to happen.

### In the Home of My Parents

Nowhere was this design more apparent, perhaps, than when it was rendered invisible. I remember the feeling of returning to my dark apartment from the airport, during my single years. Although a certain pride in my youth and independence saw me through the first few trips, it didn't take long before I would return to my parents' nearby house instead, for that lonely first night. Why? Because it was a home, not a darkened furniture showroom. There were people who cared about me, about what sort of trip I'd had, about whether or not I was tired. The house was always clean, and what clutter there was was the minimal, comfortable kind and not the kind you trip over. There were offers of herbal tea or warm milk, a fresh nightgown on my old bed, an already-heated-up electric blanket, a few good bedside mystery novels. More often than not, I could look forward to a well-stocked refrigerator full of yogurt, whole wheat bread, some inevitable leftovers from a nutritious casserole my mother had made, fruit and vegetables which I knew had been picked up at a roadside stand, and always some small wickedly chocolate "little something" hidden away in the middle of all that health. It was a scavenger hunt which never grew tedious in repetition. If there was anything even remotely affecting my physical well-being, my mother never failed to call her arsenal of Neosporin, Vaseline Intensive Care, or aloe vera plants into immediate service.

Obviously, there were many elements conspiring to make people feel good in that house, and each one represented time, thought, and work on my mother's part. Each one showed that she knew and cared about the people who lived there and wanted everyone who entered to feel good.

It became clear to me that the job of homemaking was much more than an empty progression of menial tasks, as it is often perceived to be. More than anything, I learned that the substance of homemaking is the creation of a place that makes people feel good — to, in effect, set a stage that allows positive feelings to happen. It takes great artistry to create a home where people will want to talk to each other; where they will want to linger over dinner; where they will want to snuggle up with a quilt and a book on a rainy day instead of escaping to the shopping mall. It takes skill and sensitivity to design ways to buoy, comfort, and strengthen the people we love.

## Learning to Make a Home

Yet for me, at least, the ability to make a house into a home did not just come with the territory immediately after my marriage, as I had assumed it would. Indeed, the process required considerable effort and hours of self-education. I had to learn how to make a home. And the first step in my education was trying to figure out how other people made theirs.

Why did one home embrace and comfort me, relax and cheer me, while another would leave me feeling agitated and depressed? During visits with my friends and family, I would find myself looking for clues. At first, I would just mentally jot down all sorts of disparate elements which attracted and pleased me: family pictures on a sofa table; two chairs with ottomans by the fireplace; bright, happy colors; hand-embroidered napkins on the table. But then I came to see that these elements told a story about how a family lived and how they felt in their own home. And usually I discovered that it was really the story that I found so irresistible. It was the feelings created in the home that I wanted in my own home rather than the individual objects that seemed to reflect them.

I also learned that every home seemed to carry with it its own set of expectations. And I was happiest in the homes where the expectations were the highest, and which encouraged me to be my best. On a day which did not start out well, for instance, I noticed that my environment could either encourage me to stay on a steady, downhill course or it could induce me to pick myself up, mentally set myself on a new, more positive course, and literally turn the tide on a bad day. I would rise to the expectations of my surroundings.

Recently, I was going down the stairs to make breakfast in my own home — a home which, at the time, was desperately in need of cleaning and decluttering. On the stairs, I managed to sidestep one toy, only to step on a second, and trip on a third. In the foyer, I picked my way around Lego space stations, a B-B shooting gallery, and stray game pieces from Candy Land. I passed the dining room table, in obvious need of dusting and piled high with unsorted laundry, and went wearily into the kitchen to make coffee. Suddenly, my eyes widened. The room sparkled. The floor, which had been sticky with inadequately cleaned-up spills for the past week, now shone like the morning star. The piles of school papers, junk mail, and odd receipts and stubs that always seem to accumulate near the phone had somehow vanished. The kitchen counter, which I had last really seen on the day we moved into our house, reappeared in radiant glory, and everywhere I looked there was order and cleanliness. I felt like Dorothy, emerging from the middle of her Kansas tornado and into the Land of Oz. During the night, my husband had decided to transform the kitchen himself. "I wanted it to be nice for you to come down to," he said.

But it was much more than nice. It turned around my day. Standing there in that kitchen, having just made my way through a tornado, I could feel a delightful new energy seeping into my consciousness. I felt calmer, more in control of my life, more self-assured and expectant — as if the day suddenly had possibilities which extended far beyond a simple struggle to "cope." In the midst of this newfound order, my somewhat disarrayed mind seemed to snap into action. Freed from the mountain of cleaning that I had kept pushing to the back of my mind ("I don't have time to pay attention to it right now," I would say), I suddenly realized exactly how large a portion of my energy it had gone ahead and occupied, anyway. This energy was now freed up for other things — to really listen to my children at breakfast, to take a morning walk, to get excited about a new idea. Surely this was my best, most interesting self — far more captivating than the distraught, vaguely preoccupied and weary person who had wandered down the stairs only a few moments before.

Now I am not nuts about housecleaning. But I do believe that a house which is clean and free from excessive clutter provides a stronger framework around which we are able to create a home. Cleaning house is not the body of our work. Rather it is the starting-off place which allows us as quickly as possible to get to the fun part of the job — the part in which I luxuriate; because while housecleaning may at some point become dreary to all of us, homemaking, to me, is always magic.

## Setting the Stage for Success

To practice the art of homemaking successfully, we must exercise the skills of a master psychologist. First, we must identify the continually changing physical and emotional needs of our families, and then we must try to respond to them in an unending variety of ways that will enable the people we love to go back into the world stronger than they left it a few hours earlier. Toward this end, we must assess what appeals to the senses, the emotions, the mind, and the body, as well as determine who is going to need what and when they're going to need it.

As creators of homes for our families, we daily "set the stage" for success. We choreograph the creation of good feelings by injecting a variety of personalized little gestures into the cracks and crevices of our already-crowded days. Although many of these gestures can be planned in advance, such as special parties or a regular bedtime story hour, by far the more fun and satisfying are the spur of the minute grace notes we inject into the composition of any run-of-the-mill day.

Let us say, for example, that you wake up on a rainy Wednesday. By thinking ahead to your family returning home that evening, you can picture how they're probably going to be feeling when they enter the door. How you eventually decide to respond to this day, on behalf of your family, depends in large measure on your own intuition and sense of fun. You can, for instance, start a pot of homemade soup bubbling on the stove and throw together some quick bread. You can perk up everyone's room with a tiny, special something — maybe some geraniums in your room, an unearthed favorite toy in your children's room. You might even decide to change the sheets because you know how good cool, crisp sheets will feel against the cheek of someone who's probably feeling a little crumpled and wilted.

Perhaps you are called on to interrupt an escalating conflict between two bored youngsters. So you might offer to set a generous midday fire in the fireplace and invite some of your children's friends over for some popcorn and a spontaneous "Reading Party." Or you might stop off to get a bottle of good wine, some bath salts, and a sunshine sort of movie for the VCR, which you and your husband can enjoy after dinner.

None of these actions, taken individually, is any particularly big deal. They are just little decisions, in the course of a day, which will combine to make your family feel good without their ever really being aware that anyone was consciously "doing" anything for them at all. But what a difference there is between walking into a cold, dark apartment at the end of a rainy day and walking into a bright, cozy home, redolent with the warm, husky aroma of beef-vegetable soup and homemade bread.

Why do I devote the amount of time and energy I do to all the minutiae that make up a home? First of all, I do it because I have a pretty good idea what might happen if I didn't.

## Two Dinner Parties

This past year, for example, I heard about two very different holiday dinners. At one dinner, the television blared in the living room, while the men guests all sat hunched around it, eating off paper plates on their laps, which they filled from the kitchen "buffet" table. The teenagers in the family filled their own plates and retreated, one to his room, the other off to visit a girlfriend. The women ate their meals standing up in the kitchen, complaining about the men in the living room.

At the other dinner, however, somebody orchestrated the evening differently. People sat and talked together in the living room because all distractions had been removed and the room had been made to look as inviting as possible. Refreshment trays had been placed within comfortable reach. There was a feeling of pleasant anticipation in the air as the guests caught a glimpse of the dining room table, beautifully set with its Sunday best, place cards, and a festive centerpiece appropriate to the occasion. There was a flower at each place for the ladies, as well as a small wrapped gift at each child's place, and a holiday extravaganza planned for dessert. Family traditions were all observed and enjoyed. In this home, there was much to look forward to — not just because it was "just different there," or because it "just-turned-out-well, I-don't-know-why." Ask the person who designed and mapped out the whole experience why. As effortless as happy, memorable occasions like these may appear in final form, they never really do happen all by themselves.

The second reason I devote the amount of time I do to home-making, however, is that I truly revel in the detail of my job. I am never happier than when I am buried in the thousands of widely divergent details, like Mardi Gras trinkets tossed from a full parade-worth of floats, that will enrich the lives, strengthen the characters, and contribute to the happiness of the people I love.

The fact is that there is not much that lies between us and the complete indifference of the rest of the universe — not much at all, except our friends, our families, and our homes.

## Taking On a Real Management Job

Running a home is one of the most comprehensive and demanding administrative positions to which a person can aspire. Once a mother clarifies which part of her work delights and energizes her most, she naturally begins to think in terms of objectives. And, like the manager of a small business, she embarks upon organizing the home and the family in a manner that will bring those goals to pass. Often achieving even small goals means accommodating the schedules and prefer-ences of several people or projecting both the physical and emotional needs of a particular situation in advance. Observes Linda Paxton Greer, a mother from Dale City, Virginia, who once enjoyed "a very glamorous job" with the Astronaut Affairs Office at NASA, "My 'job' as homemaker is much more demanding and requires good manage-ment skills, not only in management of people, but resources and time as well."

Elane Scott, a mother of two in Whittier, California, who lectures on "The Psychology of a Well-Run Home," points out: "Running a household is like running any other organization or system. The same general areas of responsibility apply: leadership, administra-tion, financial concerns, communication, education, and growth and expansion or goal-setting. Yet people would rather go to an office and

---

*Because I am home, I am able to teach my children those things which they will need to know that formal schooling often does not have time to cover. At the same time, I enjoy seeing the bond that my children have between themselves. And I have been a mother who has been lucky enough to see both of my children take their first steps, literally and figuratively, on the long and challenging path towards the rest of their lives. I won't be living for my children only, because I have so many other interests, but I can say emphatically that I was always there when they needed me.*

*Mary Lee Williams, Macedon, New York*

---

type someone else's memo because there is someone there telling them they made a contribution."

Because the rewards of being at home differ greatly from those we might receive at an office, it can be difficult for a mother at home to see herself as a manager, as the one in charge. In the following essay, Janet Dittmer discusses this change in perspective.

## *Am I the Manager or the Maid?*

### by Janet Dittmer

When I was a child, I didn't know anyone who wanted to be a maid when she grew up. My friends and I may have daydreamed about having a maid someday, but we certainly never considered being one.

The reasons were obvious. We didn't want a job that was considered dull, repetitive, and menial; or one that demanded hard work for low pay. To us, it all sounded pretty unappealing — being ordered around, cleaning up after other people all day long, and having only brooms and mops for on-the-job companions.

But since I've had children, I have found it much harder to avoid being a maid than I once thought. I can go around my house picking up puzzle pieces, clothes, toys, crayons, shoes, food, and books from off the floor, only to find myself an hour later picking up puzzle pieces, clothes, toys, crayons, shoes, food, and books. It seems that ordering me around is almost second nature to my children: "Find me my socks!" "Give me some milk!" "Bring me my doll!" And I really feel like a maid when everyone else in the family is lolling around enjoying life, while I'm the only one who cares how the house looks and the only one who does anything about it.

But I don't want to be a maid now any more than I wanted to be one when I was young. And I'm beginning to learn that I don't have to be one. With a change in perspective, I can be a manger instead.

Managers are respected because their work involves responsibility, skill, and tact. Managers have vision — they can see how the seemingly routine tasks of today can help an organization reach tomorrow's goals. Managers don't just decide that something has to be done; they plan how, when and by whom it must be done. Managers make each person feel valued and important, and encourage these individuals to work together for the benefit of the whole.

About Our Work

Becoming a manager, leaving my maid behavior behind, is not an overnight change. It has taken me awhile to convince myself that teaching, training, and involving children in housework as a manager is preferable to doing it alone like a maid. After all, when I work by myself, jobs are done better, more quickly, and without hearing protests and complaints ("It's not fair — my chore is harder than his chore"). But as a manager, I persist in involving others, knowing that what is being taught goes far beyond simple household tasks. We're learning about family cooperation, responsibility, and pride in a job well done — long-range benefits that are well worth the short-term inconveniences.

When I'm a manager I not only decide that a task will be done, but I also can choose which hour of the day and which day of the week to do any of my responsibilities. And only my imagination limits how I will carry them out. For example, I can do the laundry in the morning or late at night, every day or once a week. I could have children fold clothes and put them away to teach about follow-through, or I could help a young child practice matching skills using the family's socks. If I don't want to involve a child, and would rather use the laundry time as an opportunity to be alone and think, it doesn't mean that I've reverted back to maid status. I'm always the manager as long as I'm in control and each household task is what I decide it will be.

When I'm the manager, my most important responsibility is not for tasks (such as housecleaning) or for products (like the evening meal). My foremost priority is the people in my family. It's true that meals need to be cooked, clothes laundered, and the house kept clean, but I have to remember that the reason I do those tasks is to make the home a pleasant environment for my family. I want my family to understand this concept, too. They help with chores, not to please Mom or to be her slave, but because it benefits them and helps the home be a happier, more comfortable place for everyone. When people are my priority, I think of my job as one of teaching, loving, and encouraging, rather than one of scrubbing, washing, and cooking.

I have found that it's not my family who decides whether I'm going to be a manager or a maid. Rather, I decide which job I want, and my family responds accordingly. When I act like a maid, they order me around like a maid. When I act like a manager, they respect me for the perspective and creativity I bring to my job. I'm convinced that even though my children enjoy the convenience of having a maid wait on them, they are much happier when I'm providing direction in my role as manager. I'm much happier, too. When I choose to be a manager instead of a maid, I enjoy striving for long-term goals while working to meet short-term needs. It is challenging to do a job that requires foresight, leadership, and interpersonal skills. I also appreciate the teamwork, cooperation, and mutual respect I feel among family members. Trying to be a manager instead of a maid has perhaps most of all helped me understand how I relate to the people in my family. When I act like a maid, picking up after everyone and cleaning up for everyone, people are my problem. But when I serve as a manager, guiding and encouraging my family to work harmoniously together, people are my purpose.

## Special Challenges Come with a Manager's Job

A mother at home not only takes on the multiple responsibilities of a management job, she inherits the problems as well. And perhaps the first well-worn business phrase she identifies with is, "It's lonely at the top." Much of what we do at home we must do "solo." When we provide care, we have only our own personal resources to fall back on. The hundreds of decisions we face in the course of a day, we face alone. Even the multitude of questions that arise, from logistical to philosophical, are ours to answer alone. Such a great burden of responsibility can feel especially overwhelming when husbands and

---

*[My mother reared ten children] but I never, NEVER heard her complain about her workload. It would be impossible to capture in a few short paragraphs what an incredible workload it was!*

*None of us realized, as we were growing up, what a rich legacy our mother would be leaving her children. We learned from her not to expect everything in life to be easy. We learned the nobility of good, hard work. We learned the feeling of family unity, working together in the family garden, baling hay, and doing chores. Mom showed us, by example, that complaining is never a constructive answer to a problem. Her resilient optimism has rubbed off on several of us. Her consistent, God-given inner strength shows itself in each of us when we're faced with a major difficulty.*

*I will be thirty-four this fall. My husband and I are in the midst of raising our own two children. I learned a lot about motherhood from Mom. Without either of us knowing it then, she gave me the foundation for what is today a deep, unshakable devotion and loyalty to my little family.*

*I learned that motherhood calls for as much stamina, intelligence, and self-sacrifice as any profession... MORE! Because of Mom, I looked forward to being a mother some day. I pray I will leave as worthwhile a legacy for my own children.*

*Kathleen Caudill, a rural Ohioan*

---

About Our Work

children do not always seem to appreciate the sophisticated nature of what we do.

Many mothers, when beset with the same feelings of loneliness and uncertainty that trouble anyone who bears responsibility for major decisions day in and day out, turn to other mothers for strength and solace. Linda Powell Rofer, from Mission Viejo, California, writes of her first years as a mother: "A year and a half ago, I made the transition from being an academic counselor at UCLA to being a thirty-four-year-old first-time mother at home in a new community, fifty miles from friends and family. That first year was a difficult one as I began to develop a network of women friends with whom I could share the frustrations of the new experience. Through Mommy-and-Me classes and through a babysitting co-op I organized, I have managed to make those friends. And it makes a world of difference!" Writing from Albany, Oregon, Penny Snyder makes these observations about the support of friends:

"When my daughter was born seven years ago, I marveled at all the aids available to mothers. I was surrounded by baby wipes, diaper services, tippee cups, and medicine for teething pain. There were strollers with attachments for diaper bags and diaper bags with attachments for everything else. I found child care books for every stage of development and toys of every size and shape.

"After two children and many baby wipes, I now know the most important aid for mothers who stay at home. The key to a successful and happy career as a full-time mother is not a device or a book, but a good friend.

"If I had to give up all the aids I have had to make mothering easier and more rewarding, my friend is the one with whom I simply could not part. She is more important than my companion, my therapist, my confidante; her understanding and support will get me through anything with a smile."

Another executive-level problem that mothers may acquire along with their executive-level position is the temptation to become "workaholics." With a twenty-four-hour-a-day workday, our job offers no delineated respite. And since we are in charge, there is no one else to insist that we take a break.

Sometimes even forcing ourselves to take some time off isn't satisfying — in which case we are reluctant to try it again. Like the manager of a business who has no one beneath him who understands his job well enough to take his place, we can't always find a substitute who inspires enough confidence for us to genuinely rest from our labors. "I never realized how much mothers need other people to pitch in," remarks a young mother from Maryland who is expecting her fourth child. "When I have a sitter with my children, I can't relax. I'm always worried they will be too rough with the children. You can't measure someone else's understanding of children or their concept of how children should be raised."

Many mothers even express similar feelings about leaving their husbands in charge of the children, explaining that men do not seem as safety-conscious as they should be. A mother of two teens and two preschoolers describes an additional reason she talks herself out of breaks, even though her husband is willing to watch the children: "I come home after a break feeling exhilarated, then I walk in the door and ask, 'Was it worth it?' It's so exhausting to come home and start picking up. I end up having to do everything I would have done had I been home, plus my normal activities for that hour. It's like double duty."

A husband who retired early from the military for medical reasons and took over running the home for six months while his wife worked, speaks of the surprises that awaited him as a father at home:

"It would take books to describe the complexities experienced trying to meet the incredible demands of the household manager. I concluded that one person simply cannot do it — at least, not one man. A housewife is a superhuman who has the strength of Atlas, the patience of Job, the drive of a fullback, and the skills of an engineer, doctor, economist, and teacher tooled into one, plus so many other attributes that I cannot list them all.

"As a former 'Archie Bunker' type husband I now have the most deep and abiding respect for anyone who has the energy and wisdom to handle homemaking, the most challenging job I ever held. I have been a colonel in the army, a corporate officer, a successful graduate student, but none of these roles requires as much skill, dedication, hard work, and magic as being the manager of one simple little home."

◆　　◆　　◆

Though many positive surprises await most mothers when they decide to stay home, the discovery that we are not as adept at running a home or handling our children as we had once pictured troubles even the most self-confident women. What most of us eventually realize, however difficult to act upon, is that the true measure of what is accomplished at home is not reflected in a spotless house or a child who acts like an adult. Rather it lies in the making of memories and the strengthening of bonds — a process invisible to all who look on from the outside — nevertheless, a work that will influence a child's ultimate ability to rise to all that he or she can be.

*Chapter 5*

# Startling Realizations and Gentle Discoveries ...
# ... About Self-Fulfillment

As the complexities of rearing children and running a home unfold, we begin to truly understand the extent of these radical changes in our lives. It dawns on us that perhaps it will be a while before we regain complete control over our own mobility. And as we reflect upon the differences in our days since children have come into our lives, we sometimes long to go back... back to the "us" of former days.

For one thing, the old "us" doesn't appear to be all that far away. We believe that if only we could indulge a forgotten hobby or spend a little more money on clothes or get into a flexible job where our best skills would shine, then people would see the *real* us. And yet often when we do reach back and try to pull a familiar feeling of accomplishment out of its neglected resting place in our souls, something seems wrong, something seems to be missing. It just doesn't work the way it did before.

Judy Lindquist, of Nashua, New Hampshire, writes:

"Before my daughter's birth, I taught nursery school in the mornings and was a professional ice skater (teaching, coaching, choreographing) in the afternoons. I planned to continue both until the day I gave birth, and then, because even I was realistic, I would not return to teaching but would return to skating.

"When Sarah was seven weeks old, I got a call from one of the area rinks — in two weeks they were beginning work on their spring show and would I be interested in choreographing several numbers. Two weeks later I was back in the rink, my tiny baby bundled into a snuggle-pack and strapped to my chest with my husband's huge parka zipped up around us.

"It felt good to be back, teaching-creating. And I was getting a lot of positive feedback from everyone on how well I'd combined 'motherhood with career.' Would I have gotten the same encouragement had I chosen full-time motherhood? I wondered.

"After twelve weeks, I took my skates off for good. I discovered firsthand that it is impossible to 'have it all.' My decision was easy — my husband and daughter came first. I have been home for five years now and haven't once regretted it."

The fact is, we can never go back — not just because we now have inescapable responsibilities, but because we have new vistas as well. In most cases our longing to return to another time of our lives is really a longing for the mechanics of those days, not their substance. We wish we could run to the store for a bottle of shampoo without having to pack the diaper bag, locate the pacifier, and set up the stroller. We would like to be able to meet a friend for lunch without it being dependent on whether our sitter has an orthodontist appointment.

If we could return to that facile existence, we would probably do so in an instant. But few of us would trade the richness and depth of our lives now for the experience of our earlier days.

---

*I hope the pendulum is beginning to swing toward a return to the role of mother as a useful, necessary member of society. I have always been a busy person. I thought I would return to work soon after my baby was born. I thought I would be bored at home. WRONG!!!! I am as busy (maybe busier) than ever. There are plenty of activities to become involved in around my home and community.*

*However, I, like many women who worked in the eight-to-five business world before becoming mothers, have a problem. Many of my professional friends look down on me for staying home and won't take the time to talk to me and find out that I am still an interesting person.*

*Ann Riner, Texas*

About Self-Fulfillment

## Remembering the "Good Old Days"

Yet, we often find ourselves comparing our "new" lives as mothers at home with our "old" lives at the office or in the dance troupe or on the ski slopes. And our "old" lives can frequently appear more inviting. We recall how, in those days of the "real" us, we were counted on to perform certain skills, looked up to for having developed them, and congratulated whenever we excelled.

Remembering the satisfaction of those tangible rewards, Susan Bullard of Alexandria, Virginia, who is a former Air Force nurse, writes:

"I was used to the hustle and bustle of the hospital. The interaction with other professionals in caring for patients was challenging and immediately rewarding. At the end of the day, I could look back on a job well done. Furthermore, this feedback kept me going; I felt I was making a difference in those patients' hospital experiences.

"After coming home, my new job caring for my infant was not looked upon with the same importance. In fact, many of my nurse friends encouraged me to return to work. I will admit the thought crossed my mind — that I would 'regain' my feelings of importance in the workplace. Changing diapers, listening to a colicky baby, and dealing with leaky bottles was a little overwhelming twenty-four hours a day.

"In retrospect, I believe my home executive job is one of the most important things I have ever ventured to do. My paycheck is daily love and respect from both my husband and son."

In addition to our own memories of what it was like to get a real pat on the back, we are confronted daily by the media's eagerness to tell

---

*I chose to go back to work (as a medical laboratory technologist) when my children were eight and a half and eleven, and my husband (upon leaving the Air Force) didn't have a job offer. Luckily, he found one soon and working mother problems didn't seem insurmountable, so I kept at it. Now that my children are finishing up college and I am coping with empty nest syndrome, I look back on those days "cooped up" with little ones as most worthwhile.*

*The world of work has its stressors too, such as crabby bosses, office politics, plant closings, being passed over for promotion, and so on. Since I've been on both sides of the fence, I know that the grass isn't necessarily greener on the other side. Most of us can enjoy both kinds of life in sequence, as I did.*

*Cynthia Powers, near Fort Wayne, Indiana*

---

us what we're missing. They surround us with women who seem to be enjoying their hard-earned "freedom" from the constrictions of another generation. Throughout the pages of our favorite newspapers and magazines, we see enviable examples of success — some of them mothers — who have skillfully turned their educational and professional opportunities into money, title, and public esteem. Should we be out there, too?

For some of us, this kind of "success" has never had much appeal, especially when compared to the simple pleasures of rearing children. For others, however, the desire for some kind of outside achievement is not easily dismissed. If admiration for a talent or the rewards of a paycheck were once part of our daily lives, we genuinely miss them.

But the depth of feeling we have discovered for our children causes us to pause. Jan Treinen, of Scottsdale, Arizona, recounts an incident with which more and more mothers identify:

"Three weeks ago, I got a call from my former company and was offered a job — not just any job, but a job with prestige, a great salary and benefits, and lots of opportunity for advancement within the company. I left that same company some seven months ago to be home with my daughter, then fifteen months old. It was a HUGE decision then, and here I was feeling as if I were going through it all over again.

"My first thoughts were of returning to a 'place' where I could be 'me' again — to make important decisions and (try) to impress important people. I thought of the beautiful, dusty business suits in my closet and the leisurely business lunches that went with them. A second chance! Maybe I can be that supermom, just like everyone else.

---

*When [my husband and I] were married, he had two children from his former marriage, so we were an "instant" family. And me — oh, step-parenting is EASY — HA!!!! Much harder than I had expected.*

*Our children now number four, ages thirteen, ten, three, and eight months. I quit my job as a bank teller shortly after we were married and found a much harder job at home. I was forced into the adolescent and teen years without the usual upbringing. I find keeping a house a "home" is a real full-time job and frankly, I'm not sure I could handle a job outside my home as well.*

*Being a wife, mother, stepmother, and still remaining "ME" is a challenge; yes, dreadfully so, but it's also wonderfully exciting and rewarding too!*

*Marla Stuhaug, Fertile, Minnesota*

---

About Self-Fulfillment

"Then, my daughter woke from her nap. Her limp little body still warm from sleep, I cradled her in my arms, kissed her forehead, and I knew. There really was no decision to be made. I could not, ever again, leave this special warm moment to anyone else. How could I NOT choose this over cold meeting rooms and long hours working for someone else?"

Sound dramatic? It is. It's such a strong emotional tie, such a major commitment, and it comes from the heart. But it's so very real and so very important.

Somehow, after the unparalleled experience of knowing children, goals like money and power and prestige have a lot less appeal. They no longer completely satisfy us, because we have been introduced to something better, something of greater workmanship. We have caught sight of it, if only from a distance — an inner happiness that beats anything the rest of the world has to offer. And though it may take years to produce, the raw materials alone are of such superior quality, that the product is worth waiting for.

Linda Burton takes a look at this kind of self-fulfillment.

## *Finding Fulfillment at Home*
### by Linda Burton

I spent my twenties searching for fulfillment in a few rather glamorous jobs — as an actress, as a fund-raiser, and as a public relations writer. But it has been largely at home, in that most thankless of all professions — as a wife and mother — that I believe I have really found it.

Sometimes I think that personal fulfillment, like the fog, must come on little cat's feet. It is so unobtrusive and quiet that I have never really seen it coming. But every once in a while, I look up from the laundry or over my shoulder in the carpool, and there it is. It is always a surprise.

Why should this job, as creator of a home for my family, provide me with more deep personal satisfaction than I felt when my co-workers consulted my opinion fifteen times a day? Why should this job, which appears to be largely menial and is in the service of seemingly ungrateful people, provide me with anything good at all? Certainly the job has enormous frustrations and periods of boredom — even days of despair. Here, there is no witty repartee from room to room like I used to enjoy at the office — just screaming children looking for socks, unwilling to take baths, and continually accusing each other of personal injustices and physical abuse.

I suppose the answer lies in what I have discovered fulfillment, for me, actually to be. I have come to experience it simply as a feeling of general contentedness — a secure feeling of pleasant anticipation, even excitement, about the idea of getting up again in the morning. I feel fulfilled when I believe that I am using and expanding my abilities, to the best of my ability, in a way that will exert the most profound impact, carry the most real meaning, and create the greatest good in the world. Sometimes that may mean only that I am able to do a few small things, every now and then, very well.

But I am making a difference at home, and it is not clear to me whether I ever made more than the most fleeting difference in my other jobs. The skills I brought to bear in those jobs were valued, certainly, but they were not extraordinary. Lots of other people could have done — and eventually did do — the work that I was hired to do. My influence, in the limited sense that it did exist at the office, officially ended the day I walked out the door. Was that fulfilling? Did my work ever really mean anything to anybody, except in the most transitory sense? I don't think so.

When I weigh the nature of my various jobs in terms of personal fulfillment, I discover a basic irony. So much of the work I was hired to do required either that I bend the truth or that I concentrate on a set of goals and priorities that were not my own. Even though my work as an actress, for instance, certainly required artistry and honesty, I came to feel that I was only exercising those qualities in order to portray one person's version of another person's truth. That didn't seem to be enough.

The fund-raising work I did was with wonderful people and for a good cause. But there are many good causes, and the ones which I cared about most deeply, and to which I could most personally relate, either were not hiring when I was looking for a job or did not pay enough money to live on. So I did not feel a personal involvement with this work or a commitment to it, outside of carrying out the expectations of my job. Finally, in public relations work, I was — like most P.R. people — expected to put the best face on a product that was not always that attractive. "See this sow's ear, Linda?" my employer would say. "Go tell the public that it's a silk purse." Dutifully and quite naturally, I would sit down and do just that. This was, after all, my work.

---

About Self-Fulfillment

My work at home, on the other hand, is different. At home, I spend considerable time and energy telling my children that a sow's ear is a sow's ear. And I find this an infinitely more worthy endeavor. For me, the raises, the promotions, the successes, as they periodically came, never created the sense of personal fulfillment which I had believed would come with them — just a little euphoria and a lot of anxiety.

At home I continue to develop and sharpen the professional skills I used when I worked outside the home, through consulting, substantive volunteer work, and occasional part-time endeavors. That I am able to do this was one of the great surprises that awaited me when I first came home. Another was the wide array of new skills I am able to identify, explore, and develop — untapped skills which I either didn't know existed or just never had time to cultivate before. That kind of personal and professional growth represents another ingredient of fulfillment. For me, it is a critical piece of the puzzle — but only a piece.

For in addition to guiding the development of the lives of small humans, I am now presented with the greatest opportunity I will doubtless ever have to develop and strengthen my own character as well. The possibilities for spiritual and personal growth on the home front are formidable.

Daily I discover more and more about who I really am and what I honestly, bottom-line believe. My shortcomings, as I strive to be a whole person and a nice person at the same time, become crystalline. And I am offered myriad opportunities, every single day, to surmount them — the choice is mine. Sometimes, on the most frustrating and exhausting of days, I decide not to take advantage of the choice at all. I suppose it stands to reason. But the fact remains that the opportunity is there.

I do not believe that anyone can teach us who we really are more than our children. They expose our pretensions and our limits with glaring clarity, because they so relentlessly push us right up against them. And at the same time, our children challenge and expand our strengths by expecting (indeed, demanding) that we be better, stronger, kinder, smarter, more patient than we are. In terms of presenting a genuine challenge, my work at the office never even came close. In a way, it is as if our children are always calling on us to take our resources and capabilities just a little bit farther than we've ever taken them before — which usually seems to be just an inch beyond where we are certain they cannot go.

But not only do our children clarify and enhance who we are, they also insist that we be called to account for it. On behalf of our children, we take stands on most of the critical philosophical issues which have both perplexed and fascinated mankind throughout the ages. "Why am I here, Mommy?" "Am I going to die, Mommy? Why, Mommy?" "Mom, is this mine or his? How come it's his and not mine? If I just take it, will that make it mine?" "How do I get that other person to like me, Mom?"

As parents, we receive, in their most primal and ingenuous forms, all the questions which haunt the pages of all the philosophy, theology, history, and ethics books ever written. Few of us are going to respond to those questions with pat, easy answers — not without consulting the farthermost dusty recesses of our consciences to determine if those are the answers we really want to give.

The fact is that when our children approach us with those unavoidable questions about life, death, and the human condition, most of us discover that we love them too much and want too deeply to guide them accurately to respond with trite, easy answers. We are reluctant to fill their heads full of information that may have once looked good in a college blue book or that may sound acceptable in response to a Gallup telephone poll, but that we don't honestly believe in our hearts. Without the requirements and the prodding of my children, I suspect that this honest soul-searching would have come rather late to me, if at all. As it is, I believe it is largely through the discoveries we must make about ourselves and the stands we are forced to take that many of us are able to make crucial decisions about our own lives — what we want to do with them and how we want to live them. Without having consciously made those decisions, how can we ever really feel fulfilled?

It is as a result of my work at home, perhaps more than anything else, that my intentions most often strive to be noble and my efforts to carry out those intentions are most reliably marked by compassion and integrity. I can think of no effort, no work on the face of this earth, that can possibly be more fulfilling than this.

## Looking for Something Greater Than Success

No matter how certain we become that a deep and enriching kind of self-fulfillment is blossoming within us, most of us still admit to a need for just plain old success in our day-to-day lives. And if society's version of success is not what we are after, what are we expecting to find in its place?

Most of us have heard of extraordinarily devoted mothers whose children have nevertheless shunned their upbringing, even to the point of criminal behavior. Likewise, we are aware of careless and inattentive mothers who have somehow produced model citizens. Although we observe that many, perhaps most, happy, thriving adults had diligent and thoughtful mothers, we know there is no guarantee that a mother's "product" will be all that she envisioned, in spite of literally a lifetime of sacrifice and hard work.

In a sense, when we choose to become mothers, we choose to feel incompetent much of the time. For motherhood is a journey without a roadmap, a work that cannot be measured by normal standards of success. Rather, it is a work based on mutual love and a strong desire to keep trying — where the process of picking yourself up every time you falter is worth it. Whatever our original reasons for choosing motherhood, we soon learn that we are in this job for something other than success. We are after something so much grander, so much more significant. In the end, the integrity of the effort enriches us in a way that another kind of success cannot.

## Keeping Alive the "Old" Me

Though at first motherhood appears to be a rather limited sphere in terms of maintaining the skills we once had and the talents we once

---

*I have been a homemaker for seventeen years and a mother for fifteen years. I have four children and am loving every minute of it. I'm getting tired of defending the fact that I love staying home and have no desire to get an outside job.*

*It was such a pleasure to hear that there were more like myself out there. Most of my acquaintances think there's something wrong with me. Actually, it's getting to be kind of funny. It seems to be everyone's goal in life to find me a "real" job. My husband is very supportive. He came from a family where his mother was always at home, so I guess that helps.*

*I visited relatives recently in California and he stayed home from the office to be with the children when they came home from school. I was only gone for a week, but what a reception I got when I returned. There was wine and cheese, music and presents. One item was a key chain with the inscription "Wonder Woman." The next time someone asked why I didn't have a job, he jumped in with, "She hasn't got time for any more work!" I think I was missed.*

*I can't think of a more busy and fulfilling occupation than raising my children and keeping a good home. I'm involved in a million activities outside the home, of course, but my children are priority number one.*

*A mother from Middletown, Connecticut*

---

enjoyed, it becomes clear that it is, instead, replete with opportunity for not only pursuing old interests, but also developing new ones. Although a mother's first priority is to nurture her family, at home she has a lot more flexibility than at most jobs, allowing her the freedom to explore her own interests. She may have to learn to work within certain limitations (a strict budget, the school bus schedule, a nursing baby that goes everywhere mom goes), but with creativity and a little determination, a mother can definitely broaden her horizons while at home.

Writes Carol Morrissey, of West Lafayette, Indiana:

"I was not married until the age of twenty-nine, and thus of necessity was in the work force in a variety of jobs for several years. Including high school, college, and part-time employment, I've worked at twelve different jobs: driving a tractor for my dad, sorting and packing fruit in a warehouse, clerking in the college library, typing for students, teaching high school English, writing local TV commercials, making tire pumps in a factory, cashiering in a neighborhood grocery, researching for a Christian education department, writing material for same, selling Fuller Brush products, and working at McDonald's.

"Although some of these jobs are considered desirable, not one of them offered the fulfillment of full-time mothering nor the freedom I find in setting my own schedule and priorities. I'm able to develop my own skills and interests in any way that fits into my schedule. I can join organizations, do volunteer work, help out my friends, have a social life, read the newspaper, and get involved at church.

---

*It's been four years now since I've remarried and been able to be a homemaker. You see, I was one of the single mothers who had to work to put food on the table for the children and be away from home ten to twelve hours a day. Oh, those days were long-suffering, but rewarding in their own way. I'm now able to stay home and raise my four boys, ages fourteen, twelve, ten, and two. The rewards are so many, I really can't express them all so I'll just list a few.*

*One is to be able to watch each child grow and go through different stages. Another is being able to teach my own children. With the home teaching boom going on now, there are a lot of resources from which to draw. I find my creativity blossoms, and each day is fun and exciting. Although I have my ups and downs and frustrations and doubts at times, I experienced these emotions working at a career, too.*

*Donna Wooten, Fairbanks, Alaska*

About Self-Fulfillment

"I'm still able to earn extra cash by occasionally typing for college students. I can also take a little time off without feeling that we're losing money. This week, with an injured knee, I spent a lot of time on the couch (with two little boys on top of me). The only casualty of my leisure was the dirty floor."

Mothers at home are never limited by the walls of their own homes. Their world includes all that is available through the library, through university or continuing education classes, and through service outside the home. "Few of us could say we are exclusively mothers," observes Susan Tague-Smith of Albany, New York. "[If we deny] those interests which are part of our womanhood, our children would miss seeing the complete picture of who we are, both as mothers and as women."

Indeed, a mother can use the years she spends at home with her children as a time to "experiment." Through volunteer work, part-time projects, and a variety of other possibilities, a mother can "test the water" in areas she may someday want to pursue seriously as a career or simply develop as a hobby. If she discovers new skills or enthusiasm for a particular pursuit, she can continue her activities or even supplement them by enrolling in classes to enhance her new interest. If, however, her "experiment" is disappointing, she has saved herself time and effort in the future.

Janet Dittmer describes her own adventures in this essay.

---

*I am a thirty-three-year-old mother of one (a four-year-old daughter). I have been running the household full-time for seven years, after working full-time for eight years as an executive secretary. In eight short years as a career woman, I accomplished all my goals in the stockbrokerage field. I abruptly resigned to stay home — to "smell the roses" and run a household for a year or two. After that time, I was faced with the decision to re-enter the working world or to have a child.*

*I knew nothing about children; I didn't even like them. I did know how to work; I loved working. I decided to try something new. Having my daughter to rear has been the best thing that could ever have happened to me. It doesn't compare to my "old life."*

*Linda Brunner, Rochester, New York*

---

# The Most Important Things

## by Janet Dittmer

I've always pursued a variety of interests, from playing the piano to doing Appalachian-style clogging. I've also held jobs where I washed dishes, taught, did clerical work, produced visual aids, and did research — acquiring a bachelor's degree and a master's degree along the way. But when I contemplated desired vocations, my first choice was always to have a home and family.

Consequently, at age twenty-seven when I had my first baby and left full-time employment, the transition was an easy one. I thoroughly enjoyed being home with this new little son who was much more company than I ever dreamed a newborn could be. And, even though I had left a good job and very pleasant associations at work, I never drove past my previous place of employment without thinking, "I'M FREE! I'M FREE!"

As a mother, I was doing what I had imagined to be the best job in the world — and although it was a harder job than I had suspected, it was also a lot more fun. Still, influences such as personal acquaintances, the media, and my own educational background caused me to question whether this was really enough. Shouldn't I be doing something else to fulfill myself as a person apart from my fulfillment as a wife and mother? Wouldn't I become boring and have no life of my own if I didn't pursue outside interests? These questions led me on a search to find "fulfillment," even though I was very happy just being home.

Knowing I didn't want to return to outside employment, I tried a variety of other paths. First, I experimented with selling crafts. I imagined myself as a famous craftswoman — smoothly running a business while managing my home, and enjoying everyone's comments on how clever I was. However, after sewing countless baby items and entering a few craft fairs, I found how much work and time it took, how little money I made, and how much more clever most other people were than I.

Later, thinking of my possibilities as an enthusiastic salesperson, I began to sell Tupperware. I found it enjoyable to meet new people and there was never a problem finding good use for the money I earned. I also found exhilaration in trying to meet my home and family responsibilities with time and energy left for selling. But before too long, the initial excitement wore off, and one thing I knew I hadn't found was fulfillment.

A different tactic I tried was to forget about earning money and to just concentrate on developing skills. I practiced calligraphy, dabbled in too many crafts to count, and took adult education classes whenever I could. Some of the activities I thought I might like were not so fun once I got into them. For example, I took a cake decorating class and soon after volunteered to decorate a cake to serve ninety at a church social. As I worked on the cake the night before it was to be delivered, I became less and less enamored with my new hobby. I had put too much coloring in the frosting and the colors looked garish; the decorative borders were terribly amateurish; and the cake sagged precariously. At about 1:00 A.M., my husband had to physically restrain me, or I would have smashed the whole thing to put it out of its misery. Although I delivered the cake the next day, and it could have been considered "passable," my new interest came to an abrupt end.

Another time, however, a friend introduced me to the needlework skill of counted cross stitch. Ever since, I have had to discipline myself to control the "addiction" I have for the hobby or our family would never eat. Between these two extremes — disasters which nevertheless taught me about myself, and hobbies I could hardly put down — were many other experiences. But even the new skills I found most enjoyable did not satisfy the yearning for fulfillment I thought was somewhere "out there."

I next thought that maybe I couldn't find what I was looking for because I had too many interests without a specific area of expertise. I determined that I would discover "my thing," which I defined as the one area I would become identified with because I'd be such an expert in it. I had a problem, however, because I enjoyed all that I did and debated whether I wanted to give anything up just to have time to perfect one area. Finally, I came up with a solution to my dilemma. If I would concentrate on home organization and time management, not only would I have an area of expertise, but I would also be so good at using my time that I would have even *more* time to keep dabbling in all the other areas! I began reading books on organization and time management, and it has continued as an area of great interest to me. But even the discovery of "my thing" didn't end my quest.

Through these early searching years, I truly loved being home. My family kept me busy, entertained, and very challenged. But every once in a while, that nagging question would surface: "This isn't enough — what *else* are you going to do?"

The turning point for me was the day my fourth child was born. When I held that beautiful, miraculous little person in my arms, I finally understood that it didn't matter whether or not I was ever known as an expert in anything, or how much money we had, or whether or not anyone considered me clever. What DID matter was the quality of my relationships. I looked at that sweet baby and knew that nothing else would matter much if I didn't have a close, loving relationship with her — and with her brothers and my husband. At that moment, everything else seemed inconsequential compared to the possibilities I had for learning to really love.

I have looked at fulfillment in a different way since then. Before, it seemed that I was a combination of pieces: a wife, a mother, a seamstress, a volunteer, a calligrapher, a friend, a home organization expert, and so on. If I wasn't filling every role, or in my estimation wasn't performing the role well enough, I didn't think I was truly fulfilled. But now, I see fulfillment as having a central core — my relationships with others — with everything else as an addition to that center. If I am working positively on my relationships, whether or not those relationships are always smooth or perfect, I feel fulfilled. Other activities such as taking classes, doing volunteer work, or using my talents, add to my enjoyment of life and my feelings of self-worth, but are not the most essential ingredient. Before, one small piece missing from the whole would make me feel incomplete; now I know that I only feel unfulfilled when I'm not working each day to enhance my relationships.

My discovery hasn't forced me to give up the range and variety of my interests. In fact, much to my surprise, once I recognized what fulfillment really was for me, extra activities began to provide more happiness and enjoyment than they ever did before. Maybe this was because I was doing them for pure pleasure rather than for another motive like, "so I will have something I'm good at." Or maybe it was because I wasn't afraid of failing at them. If I failed, so what?

My relationships are what matter most anyway.

Even though I now enjoy my projects and activities more, my new vantage point helps me always keep them subordinate to the relationships I value most. As it says on a counted cross stitch sampler I recently completed: "The most important things in life . . . are not things."

## Women Choose To Be Home for Husbands and Selves As Well As for Children

The media seems to assume that all mothers who stay home with children while they are young eventually want to return to work when their children are older or grown. Yet many mothers find staying home offers complete fulfillment and a variety of opportunities long after the children are gone. In fact, a number of women who do not have any children choose to be home.

A mother from Wisconsin commented that she and her husband "have been happily married for twenty-eight years, raised two morally decent, hardworking, independent children, and are enjoying these years." She adds, "When women find I don't work, their remark is, 'What do you do with your time?' I always find plenty to do without TV soap operas!"

From Whitehall, Pennsylvania, Fay Neimeister writes, "Although I'm not a mother at home, I am a wife at home. I enjoy being a full-time wife, besides loving to sew, garden, cook, bake, do crafts, etc., and keep our home a 'house of order.' I'm available to be with my husband (which he has informed me he appreciates) evenings, weekends, or whenever — to enjoy each other's company and build a happy and loving marriage."

---

*I am composing this letter in the solitude of my garden. Not many jobs afford such a luxury; a lounge chair, a cloudless blue sky, and a healthy dose of Southern California sun to melt away those Monday morning blahs occasionally following an action-packed weekend.*

*I am writing because I love my work and have always felt fortunate to have had the choice to stay home. As my daughter and son mature and I watch them become responsible, well-adjusted adolescents who have both a sensitivity for others and a sense of right and wrong, I wonder what other job I might have taken which could have produced such potential.*

*In addition to their growth, I've observed my own as well in a dozen journals I've filled over the years. I've had the time to explore areas I never had the confidence to do when I was younger. Five years ago, I began taking ballet and modern dance classes at the age of thirty-three, readily admitting I had nowhere to go but up! I also have taken a creative writing class every semester and recently summoned up the courage to try poetry.*

*In all these years at home I've never been bored — quite the opposite. I'm hoping I'll take after my two grandmothers — one's ninety and one's eighty-two — because I've got so many more goals I want to achieve.*

*Donne Davis, Arcadia, California*

---

Joy Sandlund from Mt. Prospect, Illinois, was home with her children and then worked to help put children through college. After completing her "eleven-year pledge," she returned home. Joy comments, "I get a few raised eyebrows as people wonder why I would walk away from an enjoyable profession just when it could so enrich our own piggy bank. But just like the new young mom, it is a matter of priority; determining what really is important in your life. Along with eleven years' worth of cupboards to clean and weeds to pull, I have pictures to draw, flowers to plant, sweaters to knit, classes to take, friendships to nurture, problems to pay attention to, children and grandchildren to be close to, and a husband to delight. I found I couldn't take forty hours out of my week and yet be able to focus creatively on these areas as well."

Doris Schiavo of Collegeville, Pennsylvania, emphasizes how she feels she is better able to fulfill her roles as mother and grandmother because she doesn't work:

"So many of my friends say, 'What do you do all day now that your children are gone?' They don't understand that your children are never 'gone' and can always use some support. I go to my daughter's apartment to be with my granddaughter while my daughter works one day a week as a dental hygienist. I feel so happy to be able to be a real part of caring for my granddaughter. I want her to know me and I also want to experience her newly developed skills, not just to hear about them.

"Babies grow very quickly, and once that time has gone, you can never recapture it. When I had my children, I always used to say to myself, 'This must be the best age.' I'm still saying it and my daughter

---

*[I am a mother who has chosen] to stay at home and am proud of it. I haven't had a day that I've been sorry for it. I've had many compliments through the years on the behavior of my children. All I can say is that I'm sure my being there for them through each day and night has given them (and us all) a closeness and affection for each of us. Our home is peaceful, the majority of the time, and serene. My children have often commented on how different their friends' homes are. Can you believe it — they can't wait to come home!*

*It's good to know that more and more people are beginning to understand why we **choose** to stay at home with our families. By the way, my husband, who is a captain in the New Orleans Fire Department, loves me more, he says, for making this choice. He's always told me to do whatever makes me happy, and I am!*

*Sylvia M. Bruscato, Meraux, Louisiana*

About Self-Fulfillment

is thirty years old! She is such a good mother and I feel so lucky to be a part of her life.

"I think some grandmothers miss out on a wonderful experience because they are pressured into going to work just because their own children are adults. I'll probably work again someday, but for now I want my grandchild to know and love me."

## It's More Than Possible to Make Money or Keep Up a Resume at Home

Women who desire to keep up career skills, or even embark on totally new endeavors, are doing so with admirable creativity while remaining mothers at home. In fact, today's mother was raised in an era when women were constantly reminded of the wisdom of maintaining marketable skills in case they should ever face single parenthood and as a way to avoid the "empty nest syndrome." Many mothers report the satisfaction they feel when they are able to stay home and yet still contribute to their fields, keep a foot in the door, or simply bring in enough money to help the family survive financially.

Home businesses are one way many mothers have solved the problem of bringing in an income or keeping up talents while staying home with their children. A mother from Colorado, who had originally planned on going back to work, writes: "From the minute I found out I was pregnant with my son, something told me I had to stay home. I opened a secretarial service in my home and work a

---

*Before motherhood, I was employed "out there" as an office manager/administrative assistant for thirteen years. I have an associates degree in legal secretarial science/business law. I love people, organization, and working with words and paper. I also love taking my two-and-a-half-year-old son for a ride on my bike, reading him endless stories, and building pizza stores out of blocks.*

*[Not long ago] I was approached by a headhunter for a position with a lucrative salary I would love to work at (setting up a brand new office, hiring the staff, and managing the entire office). I've been home for two-and-a-half years. I love my new freedom. I am fully aware that my primary function is to teach, love, and nurture — not be a housekeeper. Sure, I like a clean house, but a few toys and books strewn around give a house that homespun, enjoyed atmosphere.*

*Needless to say, I felt flattered to be sought out by a headhunter, and I know I would derive much pleasure and positive self-esteem reinforcement holding such a position, but, NO, I won't accept the position. I've been out there, and I know I belong here. I don't even feel like there is a choice to be made.*

*Roslyn Schryver, El Toro, California*

---

maximum of eighty hours per month. Grandma takes care of my son here, where I can see him whenever I like or he can see me whenever he likes."

A mother from California, Julie Meyer, was able to combine her love for children with her love for swimming. She has a successful summer business teaching children to swim. However, the rewards are more than financial. Julie comments, "It really gives me a good feeling about myself to be able to teach young children, to watch them progress, and know that I've helped them."

When Bonnie Watkins, a mother of two children from Austin, Texas, needed to supplement the family income while her husband started his own business, she discovered that a combination of small money-making ventures allowed her to bring in the money they needed without having to find a job outside the home. She tutored, rented out breast pumps, and put on puppet shows for children's birthday parties, among other things.

The owner of a flourishing doll-making business, Andi Leopoldus of Greeley, Colorado, notes how a business at home has helped her enjoy her talents while meeting the demands of mothering a diabetic son: "Because of his condition, he needs to be watched carefully — and who better to watch him than his own mother? I have the freedom to run my own business, work at my leisure, and enjoy my children at home while having the serenity of knowing I did what I wanted by both staying at home and building an in-home business."

Working part-time away from the home, often while children are at school or when husbands can be with the children, is another way mothers continue in their chosen fields. Katharine Byrne, of Chicago, Illinois, speaks of the many years she spent in part-time pursuits: "I

---

*I stayed home and raised my two daughters. My husband was a trucker. I took his phone calls at home and scheduled his trucks. I also ran our apartment house next door. But, I was home when my children and husband came home. The kids started calling "Mama" the last steps to the door. And my husband was just as bad, calling out "Winnie." This was better for my family than what little money I could have brought in.*

*After the girls grew up I did work seventeen years for the state. I am retired now. I am sixty-two and I love being home. I do a Bible study once a month for three nursing homes. I write an article called "Grandma's Corner" for two papers. I am also helping with the Rescue Mission here.*

*Winnie Krantwashl, Grand Junction, Colorado*

---

About Self-Fulfillment

am in my seventy-first year now, and am still happy that I stayed at home — but not exclusively. I always had my hand in something besides the tossed salad and the clay for the Cub Scouts' Christmas gifts. I left the University of Chicago psychometric laboratory on my way to a doctorate, and never got back to it. But I have had the patchwork pleasure of part-time commitment to many interesting connections: writing, teaching, editing, researching; and now I am probably the city's oldest paralegal."

Many of today's mothers are recognizing that life has its "seasons"; that the talents and skills they developed prior to motherhood might be utilized in different ways during the nurturing years — then put in full gear later. The mothers of grown children who precede us often remind us that we need not accomplish everything NOW, that we can do things "in sequence." Many of them describe deep satisfaction and fulfillment that came from devoting time to their children in the early years and time for career pursuits later on. As a mother of two from Texas explains: "I am a very modern, active, and liberated woman, loving my freedom now that my children are grown because I was with them when they were growing up. I'd be the first to tell any mother she should be proud to be a mother and homemaker. There'll be plenty of time later for other pursuits! And a mother who stays home with her family now will enjoy her free time later much more, secure in the knowledge that she was there when the children needed a mother."

Though many today claim that temporarily dropping out of the work force to nurture a family can be detrimental to a career, a mother from Castro Valley, California, offers this hopeful message: "After college and a successful business career, I took thirty years off to raise four beautiful children. I can truly say that no job is as important, challenging, hard, or fulfilling as guiding a child to adulthood. I might also add that, after the last one was off to college and the nest was empty, despite the views of the media, there was no problem in

---

*My wife is now at home with our two-year-old daughter. After being at home the first year with her, my wife went back to work, and I took a six-month paternity leave to be at home with our daughter.*

*Those six months at home for me were really wonderful. I also got to see some of the frustrations and things mothers at home go through. It really is important to have some sort of support group to tell you things are all right with you!*

*Victor M. Susman, Kings Park, New York*

re-entering the business world without need for retraining or apologies."

Mothers who desire to keep up skills or earn money at home are finding ways to do it, realizing that nurturing a family does not have to mean the end of an outside career. Lynne Rasmussen, a mother from California who enjoyed a successful sales career in the electronics and computer fields and now runs her own crafts business while rearing her children at home, expresses a feeling many mothers can recognize: "I've gone from feeling 'I could never do that,' to 'maybe I could try it,' to 'I can do it,' to 'I can do anything!' It feels great!"

## Balancing Self-Growth and Family Needs Is Always a Challenge

The possibilities a mother has for developing her own talents at home are exciting; however, most of us know too well the difficulties of finding a comfortable balance between the time we invest in our own interests and the time we devote to our families. "BALANCE! Wow! What a loaded term!" exclaims Suzan Caplan, of Royal Oak, Michigan. As the mother of a young son, Suzan says, "It's been a nine-month struggle to figure out how to get the dishes done, the house in reasonable order and the two of us dressed for the day. Now I have to figure out how to be ME! It's an identity that one constantly struggles with. How in the world can I figure it out when my time is so limited by other responsibilities?"

Many of us feel guilty giving time to ourselves when, after all, we are home for the purpose of nurturing others. Yet, most of us — over a period of time, and only after much trial and error — discover that we are happier, more loving mothers when we take the time to develop our own interests. Ann Folker Antrim, of Eureka, California, speaks of the struggle to make time for herself: "It is easier in the short run to put my own needs on hold . . . to bury my own needs in taking care of others." She continues, "I've looked for all my needs to be met by being a wife, mother, and maid. But housework is never done, and I can never find self-worth in being a slave to a house. The secret to my happiness at home is for me to take time — time every day — to do a project I feel is important. The biggest challenge for me in choosing to stay home is knowing that I am responsible for creating and nurturing my own self-worth."

Like Ann, many mothers at home today are accepting the responsibility for their own self-esteem. And their solutions to the problem of balancing personal growth and family responsibilities are as varied as their different circumstances. It seems the magic key common to those who achieve the desired balance is discarding the notion of finding a magic key. Rather, success seems to rest on two qualities: the determination to keep trying a variety of combinations until something "clicks," and the flexibility to amend that "something" each time it becomes outdated as children grow older and family patterns change.

◆　　◆　　◆

When we become wives and mothers and first establish our homes, we are surprised to discover a new kind of self-fulfillment that begins to enrich our lives. These feelings of happiness seem to flow from the new person we discover when we establish relationships with a spouse and children. We find ourselves in new roles with new responsibilities, experiencing new feelings. As meaningful as this fulfillment is, however, we also want to feel that there is still just "me" — and we worry about losing our personal identity and unique attributes that we nourished before we had a family. And so, the great challenge and opportunity facing women at home today is to seek ways to enhance their own potential while keeping their family foremost in their priorities.

# Part III

# Mothers & Society: Perceptions & Possibilities

*Chapter 6*

# Setting the Record Straight

The scene is familiar because it has been painted so well for us by the media: Every morning, a majority of the nation's mothers awaken their small children in the pre-dawn hours to ready them for another day at the sitter's or at the day-care center. Every evening, these same mothers, weary but fulfilled and paid, retrieve their little ones from child care providers and return home to face an attempt at "quality time."

As a people, we worry for these mothers, who, we are constantly reminded, need more places at day-care centers than there are to go around. We worry about their children, some of whom are left in questionable care or even on their own in the afternoons after school. Most of all, we worry when we are told that this lifestyle has become the norm, the typical scene in community after community, in state after state, from coast to coast.

Although our worries for these mothers and their children are justified, our belief that they represent a majority of America's mothers is not. The popular notion that most mothers now work long hours at a satisfying job, while their children either thrive or languish in day-care, is only a myth.

## Do Labor Force Statistics Really Show a Majority of Mothers Working Outside the Home?

For almost a generation now, the media has been pointing to statistics from the Department of Labor (DOL) and telling us that mothers are leaving home. At first, news of this trend was merely a

---

surprising notation. Then, as "working" mothers became a larger and larger group, reporters began to dramatize the apparent shift from a nation of "traditional families." When mothers who worked became the statistical majority, the annual announcement of DOL statistics became a clarion proclamation of the success of the women's movement, as if the women most in bondage had finally been set free. So well-known and widely accepted have the DOL statistics become that hardly a reference to motherhood escapes mention of them — whether in news coverage, at community meetings, or in testimony before Congress.

The assumptions many of us make when we hear the DOL figures quoted seem reasonable enough. At a glance, the actual numbers give indisputable evidence that combining a job with motherhood is a fact of life here to stay for most women. The percentage of married women who hold a job and whose youngest child is between ages six and eighteen rose from 49.2% in 1970 to 74.7% in 1990. For mothers of younger children (under six years old), the increase was even more dramatic, rising from 30.3% in 1970 to 58.4% in 1990. Nor should there be any real argument with the validity of these statistics. Although prone to the same kinds of errors that plague any attempt to quantify the actions of human beings, they are the best form of measurement we have.

There are, however, grossly inaccurate perceptions about mothers and working — not because the DOL statistics are incorrect, but because of the carelessness in the way those statistics have been presented to the public. Comparing what the DOL statistics actually

---

*I'm thirty-six years old, have six children, ages nine to fifteen (four boys and two girls). I've had hard times, but I've grown. At this point, I find I feel fulfilled, youthful, informed, and very satisfied. What we "lack" in things, we've more than made up for in family pride and love for one another. I write (since 1968 when my mothering began and when my children were all babies and I was without many "outlets"); I sew and make patterns and "craft"; I am in the process of writing a child care booklet for the first year of life. I also do day-care and enjoy it! The pay isn't good, but I can fit it into my homemaking.*

*After sixteen years of marriage, my husband and I are still in love and discover something new in each other more often than I can believe. This, too, has sometimes been difficult, but we have both worked hard to find good in one another and ignore the rest. No easy task, but it does work!*

*Mary K. Rohr, Brainerd, Minnesota*

---

Setting the Record Straight

measure to what we have been led to believe they measure, yields a surprising conclusion: Many mothers called "working mothers" by the media consider themselves "at home."

## The Department of Labor Definition of "Work"

The Department of Labor statistics on working mothers are extrapolated from the results of a survey conducted by the Bureau of the Census called the Current Population Survey. Once a month, trained interviewers are dispatched with this survey to a national sampling of about 59,500 "scientifically selected" households throughout all fifty states and the District of Columbia. These interviewers ask standardized questions about the work status of all persons sixteen years of age or older who are living in the targeted homes.

Although survey information is gathered each month, figures on working mothers are only officially tabulated once a year, based on responses given during the month of March. The Bureau of Labor Statistics then estimates how many mothers are working in the entire U.S. labor force by tallying the numbers obtained from those sample households. (The survey is judged to have a relatively small margin of error.)

Because the objective of the survey is to identify trends by comparing labor force participation from year to year, the DOL has had to devise a standard definition of "employment." This definition, as printed in an "Explanatory Notes" section of the annual DOL news release on mothers and employment reads:

> Employed persons are those who, during the survey week: (a) did any work at all as paid civilians; (b) worked in their own business or profession or on their own farms; or (c) worked fifteen hours or more as an unpaid worker in a family-operated enterprise. Also included are those who

*I have two children (now thirteen and eight) whom I brought up "sans work." I found the job more rewarding and challenging than any previous job — but it did become more lonely. I started spending a lot of time thinking up shocking answers to "And what do you do?"*

*A couple of years ago, I returned to my profession on a part-time basis, working 8:00 to 2:30 two days a week. When the big question came up at cocktail parties, I found myself proudly saying, "I stay home with my children."*

*A mother from Baltimore, Maryland*

were temporarily absent from their jobs for such reasons as illness, vacation, bad weather, or labor-management disputes.

This definition clearly encompasses more than the full-time working mothers most people have imagined. According to the DOL, the 62.7% of all mothers who are usually described as "working outside the home" also includes:

### Mothers who work part-time as little as one hour per week

To most mothers, there seems to be a dramatic difference between working full-time and working part-time. In a *Newsweek* commissioned Gallup poll (reported in the March 31, 1986 issue of *Newsweek*), 1,009 women were asked whether they thought "a mother who works full-time or part-time can adequately fulfill her responsibilities to her child." Only 50% of the respondents felt a full-time working mother could do so, while an overwhelming 86% thought a mother working part-time hours could. In the same *Newsweek* poll, over half of the women interviewed who were working part-time or flexible hours "said they had cut back or changed jobs to be with their kids."

Studies conducted in 1988 and 1989 by our publication, *Welcome Home*, show that 48% of our readers earn income. Nearly 95% of those mothers do so through part-time work. Yet the part-time working mothers who write to us rarely refer to themselves as "working mothers." For instance, Diane Gates from Essex Junction, Vermont, writes: "When [my boys] started school, I went out and got a job working with special education children in a school. I see my children off in the morning, and I'm home when they get home from school. What is more fulfilling than seeing them come up with a big smile saying, 'Hi, Mom, I'm starved.' I would give no one else the privilege

---

*I'm not a mother . . . yet. [We recently moved to] Ohio, where my job opportunities were limited. To tide us over through the winter, I began to babysit. I now have a total of four babies, all within two months of age of each other, and all a joy! I feel very protective of them, and find myself bragging over their accomplishments. My husband had hoped that this would put my want to start a family of our own on hold, but it's only been intensified.*

*In being home, my attitude has changed drastically. I realize now that when we have children I wouldn't miss their growing up for the highest paid job around.*

Marcy Lilly, Columbus, Ohio

of watching my children grow. What a beautiful career, being a mother."

A California mother of two, who has continued to work part-time for a political polling firm where she used to work full-time, was surprised to discover she is officially a "working mother": "I dropped to part-time hours so I could be home with my daughter and then my son. My current superiors where I work are people I trained ten years ago when they were still college students! How can I be a 'working mother' when I have consciously sacrificed both position and salary to spend more time at home?"

While the media only rarely makes this distinction, the Department of Labor does make an effort to differentiate between part-time labor force participants and those who are in the work force full-time. Women who work less than thirty-five hours a week are categorized as "part-time." In March 1990, 16.9% of all mothers with children under the age of eighteen were working part-time.

**Mothers who work seasonally, as little as one week out of the year**

Many mothers who work do so while their children attend school and avoid employment during their children's summer vacations. Other mothers work only occasionally during the year, perhaps substitute teaching, selling handcrafts, or helping a business during a high-volume period. These mothers who work seasonally are also calculated into the DOL statistics, although some work as little as one week out of the year. According to DOL tabulations, only 34.8% of all mothers with children under the age of eighteen work full-time year

---

*Why is this profession degraded so? I have, although briefly, stayed home with my infant son and found it to be a difficult but rewarding experience. It was with mixed feelings that I returned to the office; I missed my work then, and I miss my child now. Perhaps it is a paradox, but it is commonplace.*

*The woman who cares for my son is a full-time homemaker, mother of three. My respect for her self-image and her abilities is great. Let us praise the mother at home, for she devotes herself to the future of the nation at the expense of her public image!*

*It is my hope that your organization will help to strengthen the stay-at-home mother's self-respect and confidence. She deserves the best this nation has to offer. I may one day join her.*

*Connie Mayse, Green Bay, Wisconsin*

---

round. That figure drops to 26.8% for mothers whose youngest child is under six years of age.

**Mothers who work from their homes both part-time and full-time**

One of the most common requests received by our newsletter staff is for information on how to make money at home. Many, many mothers are currently working from home, and still others would like to have that combination of extra cash and extra availability to their children. Whether working for someone else or running their own home businesses, most of these mothers have purposely chosen working from home just so they would have more flexibility in responding to their children's needs. From Ann Arbor, Michigan, Diane Spears, a single mother with three children writes: "I am doing part-time day-care and receptionist work in my home to help make ends meet. Money is tight, but I feel my responsibility is in the home with my children. I don't know of anyone better qualified than myself to raise my children — my most prized possession."

Another single mother, raising two boys in Piedmont, California, tells us: "I've been working at home as the primary provider for seven years. I didn't want to miss any of the rewards being a mother at home brings."

The Department of Labor, however, makes no distinction between women who work at an office or factory or some other facility and those who work in their own homes. Therefore, an unknown percentage of the DOL's mothers who supposedly "work outside the home" refers to mothers who work with their children around them literally *inside the home.*

---

*In today's society, which oftentimes shows so little respect for full-time homemakers, it takes guts to be just that — a full-time homemaker and mother at home. There are no regular lunch hours, breaks, and weekends; no pay raises, benefits, and bonuses; no promotions. But we do have those special joys which come in small doses — being there for the first step, the first word, the smiles, the hugs, the "I love you, Mommy."*

*I know one thing — I'll never look back wishing I hadn't missed those early childhood years. Nobody can ever take away the joys and triumphs of those very special years.*

*Dianne Jones, Albany, Oregon*

---

## Mothers who provide child care for other mothers

The women who are perhaps most astounded when they are told they are part of the oft-quoted Department of Labor statistics are those who, in order to avoid leaving their own children, provide day-care for the children of other working mothers. Both full-time family day-care providers and mothers who collect a check for watching a neighbor's child a few hours each day after school are counted in the DOL figures.

Judy Cline, a mother of two children from Newburgh, New York, is like many other family day-care providers when she sets herself apart from the working mothers she serves: "I have a great empathy and concern for women faced with options outside of the home. This empathy and love of children have led me to establish a day-care for toddlers and infants in my home. I soon realized the strain of devoted mothers and fathers having to leave their babies because of economic struggles. For many women, it is not a choice to work, but a painful fact of life."

Cindy Guzman, a mother of two from Sacramento, California, speaks of the days when she was working outside the home as opposed to her current situation as a family day-care provider in her home. She writes:

"When my first son was born, I had to start a new job — he was only four weeks old. I was very fortunate to have two loving grandmothers to care for him. It was a hard separation for me, especially since he was a nursed baby and wouldn't take the bottle (poor grandmas).

"As time went on, we both adjusted, and I even began to like my job, new friends, and lunches with my husband. I still felt that little emptiness. When my second son was born, I was once again faced with returning to work, now with two small children, and grandmas

---

*[I am] a mother and a certified nurse-midwife who works with other mothers daily. I was forced to leave my job after the birth of my son. (My partner, another midwife who was single and childless, did not want a nursing newborn in our office, nor would she allow me more flexible hours.) Now I work out of my home in my own private practice. I couldn't be happier and my son seems to enjoy meeting all my clients.*

*Linda A. Graf, North Riverside, Illinois*

---

were no longer available. I checked out doing licensed child care [as a home business] and thought if others can do it, so can I.

"My family was a great support, especially my husband. I have been home for two years now and looking back, am proud of my thriving day-care business, my steady income, and my two boys growing up at home."

**Mothers who work without pay for a "family-operated enterprise" at least fifteen hours per week**

Some mothers at home who write us mention participating in a family business. Whether or not they are paid for their work, these women are within the national definition of "working mothers." Yet, most of them are able to do their work from home or to perform their work during hours that allow their children full-time access to "Mom." Writes a former insurance agent, now the mother of one in Fort Lauderdale, Florida: "I do not have an income, but I am my husband's bookkeeper for his business, and I do many jobs that are his when I have time at home, so we can spend more time together as a family."

"Before my marriage," explains Alice Cahill of Morro Bay, California, "I did secretarial work for eight years. During our forty-five years of marriage, I have continued to use my skills at home, at first by handling typing and correspondence for my husband while he was teaching in medical school and later after he earned his M.D. degree, by being an at-home secretary in my 'spare' moments." Any time Alice's unpaid hours working for her husband at home totaled more than fifteen per week, she was technically a "working mother."

**Mothers who work full-time but have flexible hours**

Even mothers who are employed full-time can defy the media image of the working mother. By arranging flexible work hours or by having their husbands do so, many women go to great lengths to avoid leaving their children in a day-care center or with a sitter. Although they definitely consider themselves working mothers, they are usually home when their children are home. An example is Linda

---

*I recently had my first baby and am now a "family systems specialist" as one mother termed it — traditionally known as "homemaker."*

*I am forty years old and have had every type of job conceivable from Wall Street to the White House, but none as independent or rewarding as this one.*

*Karen Paull, Arlington, Virginia*

---

Hayes, a mother of two from Vienna, Virginia, who works the so-called "mother trip" as an airline flight attendant. An especially grueling assignment, which condenses a week's worth of work hours into back-to-back flights that can be completed in two days, it is nevertheless so popular that only women with nearly twenty years of seniority are able to request it. Says Linda, "It's just not in me to leave [my girls] so much of the time."

In some families where both parents are employed full-time, the husband and wife have a "tag team" arrangement: They plan their work schedules so that one of them gets home as the other is leaving for work. Thus, one parent is always available to care for the children. The DOL figures do not include information about child care arrangements. However, the Bureau of the Census has been conducting a regular survey (*Who's Minding the Kids?*) for the past several years in which working parents are asked to describe primary and secondary child care arrangements for their youngest children. In 1990, 8% of the nation's children (under age five) had "tag team" parental care.

**Mothers who are on maternity leave, whether or not they return to their jobs**

The Department of Labor definition of employment allows for the fact that some labor force participants will be home for one reason or another during the week they are interviewed. Therefore, persons home on vacation, on sick leave, or even on strike, whether or not they are being paid during their absence from work, are instructed to base their survey responses on their "normal" work week.

Women who are home on maternity leave are, according to these guidelines, counted among the working population. This would include mothers like Camille Globerman, who later decided not to return to work. From New City, New York, she writes: "I taught remedial reading to junior high students for ten years and also worked with the specialty teachers on a reading program. I now have a delightful sixteen-month-old little girl, and I wouldn't want to leave her for anything in the world. As a matter of fact, I have been on maternity leave for the past sixteen months, and now I am faced with the decision to either resign my job of $35,000 or leave my precious to another person for a ten-hour day! Even though the money is tempting, my husband and I feel that raising our daughter is more important; therefore, I'm going to resign." During her first sixteen months at home, the DOL presumably would have termed Camille a "working mother."

## The Media Version of the DOL Statistics

Once we understand that the purpose of the DOL statistics is to measure *total* labor force participation, it seems obvious that part-time workers, those who work from home, and employees on leave should indeed be included in the figures. Yet, the general public mistakenly believes these annual statistics to represent only mothers who work full-time *away* from their homes.

How did this misunderstanding of the facts evolve into such a widely-accepted misconception? And why does it matter what the public thinks about the number of mothers in the work force? Basically, the source of this pervasive misconception is the manner in which the media has handled, and continues to handle, the "working mother" statistics. Without apparent intention to distort the facts, newspeople nevertheless have created many false impressions — whether by their own misunderstanding of the statistics or by failure to use them in context.

There are at least three problems common to most media presentations of the Department of Labor (and some other) statistics:

1. The statistics are presented without explanatory information.

While the DOL statistics are widely used in discussions of women and work, they are rarely presented with any explanatory information at all. Consequently, our understanding of what the figures mean is limited to the context of the particular news report. The following facts about the statistics are almost never mentioned, yet they would significantly alter our understanding of any news report on women and work:

• As explained above, the DOL statistics are based on a survey and include mothers who are working part-time hours, who are on maternity leave, and who work from home. When newspeople introduce the statistics as the government's measurement of how many mothers "work outside the home," most readers and listeners believe the figures to be an exact count of mothers who leave their homes each day to report to full-time jobs. (Interestingly, in interviews with reporters for both newspapers and the major news networks, we have spoken with only a few newspeople who understood that the DOL statistics even include part-time workers. Rather, many reporters seem to rely on other news stories as a source for the statistics, instead of studying the actual DOL materials — which can be tedious to read and difficult to comprehend.)

- To avoid counting mothers in the survey more than once, the DOL lists each mother only by the age of her *youngest* child. Unless this fact is explained to the public, however, most readers and viewers believe that "mothers with children under the age of eighteen" means mothers whose children are *all* under the age of eighteen. In fact, many of the DOL's working mothers are women whose oldest children are grown, who have, perhaps, one teen-ager still living at home.

- Some news stories, in place of the percentage of mothers who are actually employed (62.7% for 1990), quote a slightly higher figure (66.7% for 1990). This higher figure includes both mothers currently participating in the labor force *and* those who are unemployed but who are looking for jobs. Again, it is the rare newswriter who takes the time to explain that 4% of the women in this statistic desire employment but are presently at home.

2. The context of some news stories gives the wrong impression of what the statistics mean.

Also contributing to the public's misunderstanding of today's working mothers is the use of the DOL statistics in a restricted context. For instance, when a reader is told that "58% of today's mothers work" in an article that interviews mother-doctors, mother-lawyers, and mother-bankers, an impression is left that this 58% must be mostly mothers like those in the article — who, of course, are only a small percentage of today's working mothers. Similarly, many articles on latch-key children and the debate over child care begin with a statement such as, "According to the Department of Labor more than half of today's mothers now work outside the home." This conjures up visions of half the nation's mothers leaving their children alone or in institutional care for most of each workday. In actuality, only a minority of the working mothers in the DOL statistics fit this image.

The context of many news stories also feeds the misconception that these statistics measure only full-time employment by giving the impression that a mother is no longer included in the DOL statistics when she leaves full-time employment for non-traditional work arrangements. A typical example is one article from *The Wall Street Journal*[1] which cites the DOL statistics to document the increasing involvement of mothers in the work force. Noting that "this greater commitment to work outside the home has created agonizing dilemmas for the mother who is genuinely devoted to her children but who is not Wonder Woman," the article goes on to suggest that some women might want to consider quitting their jobs to start home businesses. When the idea of starting home businesses is presented as a contrast to the mothers with a "greater commitment to work outside the home" (those in the statistics), the incorrect impression is given that mothers who work from home are not counted as working mothers. In fact, women who apply the home business solution to the work/family dilemma are still among the working mothers cited in the article's statistics.

3. When statistics are presented, emphasis is placed on mothers who work rather than mothers who stay at home.

A reporter has a choice of emphasis whenever a statistic of any type is included in a news story, and his or her decision will strongly influence the reader's assessment of what that statistic means. Today it is common to read a statement such as, "Half of the nation's mothers with children under the age of three hold jobs," when one could just as well state, "Half of the nation's mothers with children under the age of three still stay home, in spite of a growing trend for women to enter the workplace."

The March 31, 1986 cover story of *Newsweek* gives a more dramatic illustration of how emphasis can color the interpretation of statistics. Within the text of the article we read: "It's not that women don't want to work. They do — in fact, even mothers at home say they would prefer to work. According to a *Newsweek* poll done by The Gallup Organi-

---

[1]"Torn Between Family and Career? Give Birth to a Business" by Jennifer Roback, *The Wall Street Journal*, November 14, 1983.

zation, 71% of the at-home mothers surveyed said they would like to work. A total of 75% of working mothers also said they would work even if they didn't need the money."

A few pages later, the detailed results of the Gallup Poll are presented in chart form. *Newsweek*'s 71% of at-home mothers who "say they would prefer to work" was calculated by adding together the responses of women who said they would like to work full-time, flex-time, part-time, and from home. In fact, only 9% of the nonworking mothers interviewed said they would like to work full-time regular hours. Fully 91% of the poll's at-home mothers indicated a preference to be at home at least part of the regular working day, a figure which gives a completely different impression than the figure quoted in the text of the article.

Meanwhile, although the text states that 75% of working mothers would keep their jobs even if they did not need the money, the chart showed that only 13% of those interviewed wanted to work full-time regular hours! In other words, 87% of the poll's working mothers would prefer to be home *during at least part of the normal working day*. By far the most preferred category was part-time work (34%), and more working mothers wanted to quit work completely (16%) than wanted to work regular full-time hours. By choosing to emphasize mothers wanting to work, *Newsweek* completely overlooked the Gallup Poll results that showed the strong desire mothers have to spend more time at home.

## The Impact of This Statistical Misunderstanding

Unfortunately, misunderstandings rooted in the misuse of the DOL statistics have been far-reaching. First of all, the media itself has not been inclined to speak for, to, or about a population they believe to be a dwindling minority. Even today, a publication oriented to the daytime homemaker and mother — or one that even acknowledges her existence — is difficult to find.

Secondly, advertisers and businesses, conscious of the "bottom line," have not wanted to risk selling to or manufacturing for a population they believe isn't there. For the past two decades, mothers at home have often had to purchase clothing, health care products, appliances, magazines, and homes that were designed around the needs of the working woman.

This public and cultural neglect has led to feelings of isolation and frustration, such as those expressed by Collette Leskovyansky of Kutztown, Pennsylvania: "So many articles about everything (cooking, real estate, architecture) seem to mention only the two-career family. I feel that this kind of exclusion of mothers at home only reinforces isolation." She adds, "I think that what the media has accomplished for me is to infuse a sense of despondency about becoming a mother." Such feelings have led some women to return to work simply because they felt completely alone.

However, the most frightening result of misunderstanding the DOL statistics has been in the area of public policy, especially regarding child care. Although the DOL's statistics on working mothers include women who participate in the labor force in a variety of ways (not just full-time employed mothers or those whose job circumstances dictate the need for child care), the notion persists that every working mother needs substitute care for her children. This mistaken assumption has led many well-intentioned people — from community leaders to reporters to politicians — to routinely misuse the DOL statistics as "proof" of the need for more child care.

The truth is that all of the widely publicized estimates on how many children need child care are derived from formulas based on how many working mothers are "counted" by the DOL. Yet in reality, many mothers who are considered an active part of the labor force do not need any child care services at all. It is important for the public to understand that estimates of child care needs based on the DOL's employment statistics on mothers are both inaccurate and misleading.

Unfortunately, other methods of accurately measuring child care needs either do not exist or have not been designed by researchers or discovered by the media. Possibly the most reliable indicator of child care trends across the nation is the aforementioned Bureau of the Census report, *Who's Minding the Kids?* According to this report, most children over the age of five are actually in school the entire time their mothers are at work. Children who require secondary care (before and after school) arrangements or whose parents work during nonschool hours are mostly cared for in their own homes and/or by relatives or friends.

The majority (60%) of preschool children (under five years of age) are cared for by their own parents: 47% have a mother at home, 5% have a "doubletime" mother (who earns an income while caring for her children), and 8% have "tag team" parents (mother and father share care between themselves). In addition, 11% are cared for by relatives, bringing to 71% the number of young children cared for by their families. Of those preschoolers who do have substitute caregivers, 12% are in family day-care, 14% are in center-based care, and 3% have a child care provider in the home.

This report indicates that the number of children under the age of fifteen in need of non-parental care may be far from the majority. However, even a survey of how children are cared for today is only a measurement of current use, not a statement of need. Until further research is done, *no one* can provide an accurate assessment of how many of the nation's women who are described as "working" mothers really need or want substitute child care for their children.

Meanwhile, several public opinion polls taken during the late 1980's and early 1990's began asking parents about their desires concerning the care of their children. Some recent examples of these surveys are:

• A 1987 Cornell University study found that two-thirds of all mothers employed full-time would like to work fewer hours so that they can devote more time to their families.

• A 1988 *USA Today* survey found that 73% of all two-parent families would have one parent stay home with the children if "money were not an issue."

• A 1989 Lou Harris poll found that eighty-two percent of the American public believe it is best for young children to be cared for by one or both parents or by extended family members.

Other polls demonstrated similar results. Clearly, most parents would prefer to rear their children in their own homes.

♦   ♦   ♦

The message widely reported from the DOL statistics is largely a true one. Mothers today are indeed participating in the work force in record numbers. There are more mothers than ever solely responsible for the economic well-being of their families or jointly responsible where a single income will not make ends meet. There are also more women with careers they want to pursue and educational background they want to utilize.

But there is another message hidden in these statistics that is not widely reported, and which the prevailing reports sometimes mistakenly deny. It is that mothers continue to make great efforts to spend as much time with their children as possible. Not only do millions of mothers resist social and economic pressure and remain outside the work force (full-time homemakers still represent the largest single occupation category among American adults), but also millions of DOL "working mothers" participate in the labor force in creative and non-traditional ways just so they will be available to their children a majority of the time.

The Department of Labor statistics, as misinterpreted by the general public, daily influence decisions in millions of homes, in thousands of business establishments, and even in local, state, and federal government policy. Since these decisions are literally shaping the future of the country, it is imperative that the statistics be properly understood.

*Chapter 7*

# Opportunities for an Enterprising America

**M**edia coverage for the past three decades has almost universally divided mothers into two distinct camps: mothers who are home with their children (pictured as a shrinking minority) and mothers who "work outside the home" (identified as the growing majority). Mothers at home are supposedly politically conservative, married to high wage earners, and ideologically committed to the view that women belong in the home. "Working mothers," on the other hand, are depicted as educated women pursuing self-fulfillment in the workplace and mothers forced to work for economic reasons.

The outpouring of letters we have received over the years, from mothers of nearly every political, religious, and socio-economic background, completely contradicts this picture. We have heard from low income and single mothers who have managed to stay home, women with high incomes who feel they "must" work, political conservatives who have balanced career and family for years, and ardent feminists who quit work as soon as their first child was born. Thus we have learned that mothers simply cannot be categorized by their work/home choice.

If anything unites mothers today, it is not the choices they make concerning the care of their children; it is the exhausting inner turmoil they suffer as they weigh the alternatives. Pushed one way by an intense social and economic pressure to work and pulled another by a dawning realization that they are truly needed by their children, most mothers feel hopelessly torn. In fact, many of them wander in and out of the work force, seeking the support they need from a society that is only just beginning to realize how to give it in either place.

Certainly, the extreme stereotypes of the seventies and eighties have done a real disservice — both to mothers who work and mothers who stay home. We are now in the process of discarding these outdated images so that mothers will at last experience significant changes in their daily lives. However, two major hurdles remain to be cleared before mothers truly will begin to feel the support of the society in which they live.

First, we must realize that mothers who work and mothers who stay home have more in common than they have to argue about. And second, we must consciously improve the public understanding of the stresses on today's mothers so that we can respond sensitively to their needs.

## The Alleged War between Working Mothers and Mothers at Home

One of the consequences of the damaging media stereotypes which we have endured for so long has been the polarization of some mothers. In an effort to live up to many of these unrealistic images, mothers have been at times influenced to take sides against each other, in spite of their common concerns about motherhood.

Every so often a rash of newspaper and magazine articles, and even some television talk shows, spotlight what they term a "war"

---

*I am the mother of four. I made several complicated decisions as I raised my four children at home to ensure that I could, along with my husband, be the primary people in our children's lives. The economic situation in this country, particularly in the Washington, D.C. area, did not make it easy for me to make the choices I did.*

*While raising my children, I attended college part-time in the evenings to earn a B.A. degree and then an M.Ed. in early childhood education. My studies have helped me understand more fully the economic plight of a diversity of populations in this country. I have been sensitized to their needs so that I have spent much time thinking about day-care and other services needed by many of our families.*

*It is my belief that a change in attitude toward the importance of the family is needed as well as a change in attitude that alternate care for children is the only answer to our economic situation. It is not.*

*Pat Kinney, Fort Washington, Maryland*

---

between mothers who work and mothers who stay home. Sporting titles like "Mothers Against Mothers" and "Mom vs. Mom," they report the hostilities that surface when women who make different choices have to deal with each other on a day-to-day basis. (One magazine even went so far as to illustrate its story with photographs of two mothers in boxing shorts and boxing gloves slugging it out in the ring.)

These stories play up the impasse that has allegedly developed between the new "typical" mother, who goes off to a job every day, and her more "traditional" sister who stays home. The articles outline the logistical problems of trying to get these mothers to cooperate on those details of their lives which force them into contact with each other — such as carpooling and assisting at school programs, scout meetings, and athletic events. Replete with quotes where each set of mothers complains about the insensitivity of the other group, the articles usually stop short of name calling, though the impression lingers that the names would be there if it were not for the good taste of the writer.

---

*I am disturbed that in these times I must apologize for this career choice to so many of my fellow feminists. I do not spend my days wearing a professional title, but I wholeheartedly support those who do. While many of my contemporaries dash off to climb the corporate ladder, my days are spent singing "London Bridge" in the sandbox or trying to convey the message that the stove is hot when the carrots are steaming. I am proud of my work, and I am hurt by the responses such as, "I'd go crazy if I stayed home," or "You must keep up with all the soaps." Such an image should have died along with the myth of the "dumb blonde."*

*The fact that many people maintain this misconception is not surprising, however. It is perpetuated partially by the advertising industry which makes it difficult to turn on the television and avoid being trapped in a world of stereotypes. Women are too often presented in two extremes: superwomen who hold down the corporation, rush home to a spotless house, and fix a gourmet meal while still looking sexy for their men; and women who panic at the thought of someone removing their fabric softener or who lose sleep over not removing "ring around the collar."*

*I firmly believe women can and should be whatever they desire. Although we must continue to fight to achieve that constitutionally guaranteed right, we must fight the system and not each other. We must not allow ourselves to be torn apart by the stereotypes we are fed.*

*Sheila D. Luftig, Hatboro, Pennsylvania*

Working mothers tell of nannies being shunned socially by at-home neighbors and of the organization of playgroups exclusively for the children of mothers who stay at home. They describe the elaborate promises they feel forced to make every time they miss a turn carpooling or need a neighbor to babysit on a surprise "snow" holiday from school. Meanwhile, mothers at home relate stories of double duty volunteer work; of handling Brownie and Cub Scout troops single-handedly; picking up someone else's sick children from school, letting other people's plumbers into other people's houses, and collecting a neighborhood's worth of UPS packages during the pre-Christmas season.

Certainly, such incidents have taken place. Certainly, there are neighborhoods where such ill feelings seem to have become the rule, and where employed mothers and mothers at home try not to cross paths.

But the truth is, these articles are about something that happens to the majority of us a minority of the time. These incidents, many of them based on misconceptions in the first place, are merely the natural frictions that arise in any situation where busy people with common goals but different points of view must compromise for the benefit of both parties. The same kinds of episodes take place in most offices, in most governments, even in most churches all over the world.

---

*Now that I am no longer a "working mother," people react to me in ways that make no sense. I feel a real loss of respect. People tell me I'm wasting my education by "not working." In other words, if I were running a day-care center, taking care of other people's children, doing the same thing I am doing now with my own kids, I would be considered a career woman who is using her education and contributing to the economy. If, while running this day-care center, I were to pay an expensive nanny to come to our house and give our children the attention and care I now give them, both the nanny and I would get more respect than does a mother staying at home!*

*I have a great deal of respect for career women. My mother worked from the time I was a young child. Although it was hard on her, she was able to manage things with our extended family, friends, and neighbors, as well as a good day-care center, so that my brother and I did not suffer. I respect women who manage their lives, either by necessity or by choice, so that they can work outside the home and still raise families. All I ask is the same respect for women who choose to stay at home.*

*Lynn Donahue Proegler, Ann Arbor, Michigan*

Clearly, anyone who wants to spotlight jealousy and resentment can find women who will gladly criticize someone who lives a different lifestyle. Nearly every mother can recall a time when "the other mother" caused her to feel hurt and angry. Yet women experiencing such feelings are not necessarily ready to do battle. It is the media's very display of the problem — their atmosphere of selling ring-side seats to a mud fight — that escalates common personal struggles into an artificial "war."

The fact is that last year's working mothers may well be this year's mothers at home and vice versa; that many women have experimented with both choices and understand the challenges and satisfactions of both worlds. No matter where they "work," most mothers' hearts are in the same place — at home with their families.

## Mothers Need to Feel Welcome in Our Society

"Families are the basic unit of a society," writes Martha Aliperti, a mother from Centerport, New York. "A stable family life is necessary and vital to the health of a nation. Mothers contribute to this stability. Motherhood must take the important place in society which it deserves. No one need apologize or explain their choice in following this vocation."

But America's mothers do feel the need to apologize. While our society claims to honor motherhood, our daily lives tell quite a different story.

Every mother can recount some shocking story of blatant mistreatment by someone in a public place who was offended by the very sight of her children. But as unsettling as such experiences are, they are not the main source of the frustration many mothers feel as they try to function in American society. Rather, when a woman becomes a mother, she begins to experience a subtle kind of neglect, an unintentional thoughtlessness that manifests itself in hundreds of small ways, as she goes about her routine, daily business. It is standing in line at the grocery store with an unhappy toddler when no one offers sympathy or assistance; it is eating out in a "family restaurant" and finding no place to change a diaper without laying the baby on a dirty floor; it is a mother asking the pediatrician a question based on *her* observations of *her* child only to have the doctor dismiss her concerns. And this neglect is felt in many apparently insignificant instances, such as waiting rooms without toys, aisles too narrow for strollers, drinking fountains too tall for children, and restaurants with high chairs (if any) in disrepair. It stems from an overall, matter-of-fact feeling everywhere she goes that no one, after all, expected her to show up with *children*.

But a mother must go about the details of daily life just like anyone else. She has to buy food, purchase clothes, go to the doctor, fill prescriptions, renew her driver's license, mail packages, and carry out all the same obligatory tasks as everyone else. For most mothers, however, the complexities of day-to-day living are multiplied. First, she must often add to her own routine errands those of her children. Second, rather than proceeding quickly and efficiently on her own, she must often bring her children along with her.

As unrealistic as it is for cashiers, store clerks, doctors, pharmacists, postal clerks, and others to expect a mother to avoid ever going out in public with her children, business establishments and other public places are rarely prepared to handle the reality of children. Not only does this make the handling of children more difficult, it also puts added pressure on mothers who then feel obligated to worry about whether their children are intruding on the solitude of the surrounding adults. In addition to carrying out her errands, therefore, a mother is likely to be worrying about keeping her children entertained, keeping them quiet, keeping them still — all while negotiating places not always fit for strollers or curious little people. While many mothers have older children to help out or are usually able to manage by themselves, many others find dealing with the "little things" in life both complicated and exhausting.

Both mothers who work and mothers who stay home know the many stresses associated with handling children within the framework of this society. In the following essay, Linda Burton explains how these stresses are intricately related to our "bad days."

# The Bad Days

## by Linda Burton

There is a Greyhound bus in my imagination, which I dream of taking on the bad days at home. On the moderately bad days, I plan speeches and theatrical exits. But on the awful days, all I want to do is quietly, in an ordinary sort of way, tell my family that I am going to the store for a loaf of bread; then walk out the door, drive carefully and purposefully to the Greyhound bus station, and never even look back.

Where would I go? It doesn't really matter. Maybe start life again in another town, under some other name. Maybe be a waitress in a quiet little diner and have a quiet little apartment and two or three little cotton dresses and never again have to... have to, what?

I suppose it depends on the day. Never again have to respond to the ninety-third request for some form of sugar in the same four-hour period; never again have to mediate twenty-six conflicts in rapid succession; never again have to completely clean up a room which I had just completely cleaned up only two hours before. Never again have to cook a dinner which is almost never good enough. Never again have to work hard under a barrage of criticism, complaints, and demands.

The thought is intoxicating. And on the bad days, the idea of escape lures me like Bali Hai.

I once asked my mother if she had ever had any truly bad days when my sisters and brother and I were growing up. Of course, I knew that there had doubtless been some days that were horrible — there must be for every mother. Yet, somehow I couldn't really believe that she could have experienced the degree of despair which I periodically do.

She recalled how, when we were small (as my children are now), we would go as a family to the beach for a week or two. Because my parents had very little money at the time, we would stay in a two-bedroom, tiny little cottage about a block-and-a-half from the ocean. My mother was expected to bring all linens, cooking utensils, and food, and to essentially carry all of her work from home to the beach. For me and my siblings, it was a great vacation. For my mother, I think it was probably only a compression of the demands made on her into a smaller, less hospitable place. One night, she said, she went to the beach. She sat on the shore, watched the ocean, and wept. She told me how she cried there because she had felt that she couldn't cry in the cottage around us and my father. And how she prayed that the ocean might just silently come and get her and wash her away with it.

No dramatics, no yelling, no accusations. Just wash her away. I have probably never felt closer to my mother, nor more empathetic, than when she told me that story. Eventually, she told me, she turned around and came back — back to the cottage — though I think she was never entirely sure why. It was just something she did, like the interminable laundry.

## Why Do We Have These Bad Days?

What is it about the business of being a mother that must almost necessarily bring us to these occasional times of exhaustion and despair?

First at fault, I think, is the vast, limitless nature of the job. Mothers are literally at the job — often hard at work — twenty-four hours a day, seven days a week, with no coffee breaks, lunch hours, or sick days. When we vacation, if we vacation at all, we are usually required to bring much of our work along with us. In any other profession in this country, these working conditions would be considered well below the level of accepted human endurance.

But it is not just the shifting parameters of her job that can bring a mother right to the edge. There is also the incessant nature of her work. With all of its unparalleled rewards and excitement, the nature of a mother's work, like most work, does have a dark side. And when this dark side of the job is joined by the feeling that her days have no end, a woman can easily believe she has come to the end of her rope.

Like Sisyphus pushing his rock up that legendary hill, a mother, at one time or another, will feel that no matter how much she has done, someone has always come along right behind her and undone it; that no matter how hard she works, there is always more to do; and that no matter what she has managed to get done, it is never good enough. For most of us, there is eternal cooking, cleaning, breaking up fights, carpooling to the same places and back again, putting the same clothes in the same wash and taking them out again. On the bad days, it is easy to forget that these repetitive, interminable chores are only a small part of an otherwise pretty fascinating job. Most of the time, these repetitious tasks are simply taken in stride as incidental to the real work we do. But on the bad days, the repetitious tasks consume us. They become, in our minds, all that we do.

## And the Relentless Demands...

We must add to this the fact that these endless tasks are punctuated by the ceaseless battering of children's interruptions and demands. Few people, I think, other than the mother directly involved, can ever be truly aware or completely understanding of the emotional toll which these demands eventually take.

Recently I was working under deadline to finish a piece of writing. My younger son interrupted me with a request — the same one he had made many times that afternoon — for some juice.

"Mommy, I want some juice," he said.

"You just had juice," I responded. "I've gotten it for you already fourteen times today."

"Get it, Mommy," he whined.

"I can't now, honey," I said in what I thought was a sweet tone of voice. "My hands are very busy. I'll get you some more in a few minutes."

"I want it now, Mommy," he rejoined.

"I know, honey. Just a few minutes." A ten-second interval elapsed as my son went into the other room, picked up a toy and threw it down again. He returned.

"Has it been a few minutes, Mommy?" I smiled (which I thought was a pretty incredible thing for me to be able to do at that point).

"Not yet. Honey, leave me alone for a few minutes. I am right in the middle of this, and I am losing concentration."

"Mommmmmeeeee," whined my son, "I want my JUICE."

"No. I can't now. Get some water if you're that thirsty."

"I don't want water."

"If you're thirsty enough, you'll drink water."

"I AM thirsty. I'm THIRSTY. But I'm not thirsty for water, I'm thirsty for juice."

At this point, I managed to recoup my fading maternal strength and attempted one kind, but final, parry. "Now leave me alone for a minute, honey." My son returned the favor with a forward thrust.

"I waant juice. I want juice, juice, juice, JUICE."

"STOP IT!!" I cried. At this point in the conversation, the phone rang. I was forced to make quick apologies and promises to call back, while my son screamed in the background. I stormed angrily out of my chair, jerked open the refrigerator, and got the juice, poured it, and put it in front of him. "THERE!" I said. "There's your JUICE!" I stormed back to my desk and tried to pick up where I had left off when I heard my husband, returning from work, at the front door. Before he had a chance to say hello, my son let out a devastating whine.

"I didn't want APPLE juice; I wanted ORANGE juice!" I shrieked in frustration, which was met with loud tears at the kitchen table.

"For heaven's sake," my husband remarked calmly, his comforting arms around my sobbing son, "he only wanted some orange juice. Don't you think you're overreacting? Here, honey," he said, "I'll get you some orange juice."

Now much of the time, my husband is one of the most remarkably understanding and insightful of people. He is extraordinary. But on this occasion, I felt as if I was beating my brains out on the tennis courts at Wimbledon, and my husband was sipping tea in the Royal Box and wondering why the players were sweating.

## "If You Don't Come In at the Beginning, Don't Criticize the Play"

Our stresses as mothers are multiplied when the pressures that create our tensions are misunderstood or — as is more often the case — incompletely understood. As any critic will tell you, if you want to accurately assess someone else's performance, you have to come in at the beginning and sit through the whole thing.

Most of us who catch up with a mother on one of her bad days not only make assumptions about the quality of her life, but also make instant judgments about her fitness as a mother, based on the same kind of incomplete information. Most of us, as my husband did with the orange juice, come in near the end of the story.

Sometimes, while out shopping or on the street, I will see a mother say or do something hateful to her child. "How many times do I have to hit you before you listen?" or "Sit DOWN, do you hear me?" while shoving a child angrily into his seat. Or I have seen a mother give a child a hard whack on the bottom, screaming at him for "going where I couldn't see you!"

From the view of the passerby, these angry outbursts can appear unprovoked and cruel. The most disgusted among us whisper to each other and consider calling the child welfare authorities. "How could this woman do this to her child?" "Why did she ever decide to become a mother, anyway?" "Some people just shouldn't have children." Young single women who happen upon one of these angry mother-child exchanges look on disapprovingly and whisper to friends about how they can think of nothing more frightening nor horrible than being a mother at all, let alone "one like that."

Opportunities for an Enterprising America

And yet those of us who have been mothers are more inclined to wonder: How many times did that mother try to explain something to her child and try to explain and try to explain? And how many times did the child ignore her, refuse loudly and rudely even to listen to her multiple attempts at kindness and reason? How many times? How many times before her best intentions and Herculean efforts were simply exhausted? Or how many times had the mother nicely reminded her child to sit down before WE ran into her? How many times did she see him fall and hurt himself because he was standing precariously when he should have been sitting, before she finally pushed him and shouted, "SIT DOWN!"

I am convinced that most of these passing mothers are not child abusers. They are just good women who have taken it and taken it and taken it until they could literally take it no more. They are women who desperately need a break and don't see one in sight.

## Looking for a Break

Some people would, I know, contend that life at home has always been this way — that the stresses of mothering and the nature of a mother's work just come with the job, and we should stop complaining and just make the best of it.

However, it is extremely easy to forget that until only very recently, mothers at home with their children have had relief built into their jobs in one form or another.

What is new today is the startling fact that most of the established avenues of relief for mothers, common even into the 1950s, have all but vanished. This age is one of the first in recent history where mothers have had almost no control over their own ability to take a break.

I realize, of course, that every generation has its own set of complaints and its own burdens to bear. Our grandparents, for instance, did not have disposable diapers, convenience foods, the polio vaccine, or a host of other improvements which are now a commonly accepted part of everyday living. But most of them did have more available help and extended family living nearby — frequently even in the same house, a community full of other mothers at home for support and company, stores that delivered and doctors who made house calls. What seems to today's mothers as luxuries from a nostalgic and sentimental past were everyday realities to mothers just a little over a generation ago.

## The Newest and Worst Stress

In the not-so-distant past, even mothers who were unable to hire help or did not have family living nearby were usually able to take a cheap, easy break called "Go outside and play." Whenever my own mother had guests over or whenever we children had simply become too much for her, she would wipe her brow, sigh, and say, "Go outside and play." Out we would go. Similarly, when our mothers needed to run errands, they would order us to "wait in the car until I come back." We, as children, had independence and mobility in a way that many children today clearly do not.

What mother — particularly mothers living in or near a major metropolitan area — could tell her child to "wait in the car until I come back" today? Or would even consider doing it? Very few.

For mothers today have to contend with a brand-new stress: the frightening and widely publicized epidemic of missing and exploited children. In the past several years, a multitude of converging factors have been bombarding mothers with the message to "stick with your children and don't let them out of your sight." The message is everywhere, from faces of missing children on grocery bags and milk cartons to television specials, videotapes, books, and newspaper accounts. Is it any wonder that a mother would occasionally, hysterically scream at her child to "Stay right where I can see you, and don't move!!!"?

Many of our small children do not go outside and play unless we are right on top of them. When we get in and out of the car to run the many obligatory errands which running a household requires, our children get in and out right along with us. No matter how many times we laboriously have to haul them in and out of the required seat belts or carseats, no matter how tiring the littlest one becomes on our hip; no matter how hard it is to keep an eye on several children in a store and still make the wisest choice of merchandise — we have to do it. I recently heard a friend exclaim that at the end of the day, "My eyes feel like Marty Feldman's!" — eyeballs running around in their sockets like drunken goldfish which had just been required to swim the English Channel. I know that the actual toll that these new exhortations for eternal vigilance must daily take on a mother is hard to reckon. But based on personal experience and much firsthand observation, I believe it is immense.

## Searching for Relief

What's to be done about this? I believe that mothers today would have measurably fewer bad days if some of the old avenues of relief could be creatively restored to their lives and some innovative new avenues opened up. Today's mothers, in my opinion, are much more in need of relief at home than they are in need of additional work outside the home. And I believe that we will create imaginative change in our communities, seek out sensitive accommodations from retailers, and build renewed understanding for our motherwork throughout our society.

On whatever bad days lie ahead, I hope we will concentrate our energy on helping to effect these changes instead of on feelings of internal inadequacy, when we don't know where to turn.

## Businesses Begin to Respond to Mothers

Already, exciting changes are occurring around the country which will ease the burdens on today's mothers and which carry the promise of impending dramatic changes in the quality of their lives. Some have been initiated by mothers themselves; others by canny retailers and industry executives who covet their business; and still others by people who, quite simply, care very deeply about the quality of life we are providing for America's children.

Over the past several years, more and more retail businesses have created play areas where children can entertain themselves while their mothers shop. It has become increasingly common to see public bathrooms with diaper-changing facilities, stores with play areas, and built-in safety belts on the childseat of grocery carts. Some supermarkets even have child-size carts for children to push alongside their mothers.

Other smaller gestures mean just as much to mothers. For example, in Rehoboth Beach, Delaware, a chain of gift shops, The Sea Shell Shops, displays a paper cut-out of a child's hand on which is written: "Little hands are always welcome here" — a particularly meaningful welcome since the shop is full of fragile items. In Vienna, Virginia, a small paint and wallpaper shop called Tri-City Too places its counters with shelves of pattern books in a neat rectangle in the middle of the store to form a cozy play area for children. Mothers can browse through wallpaper books at the counters while their children play right in front of them inside the contained area.

Giant Food, an eastern supermarket chain, offers a "candy-free" check-out aisle in every store. Ben Franklin craft stores invite mothers of small children, pregnant women, handicapped persons, and senior citizens to shop at sale prices the day before any actual sale, allowing them to avoid the crowded aisles on the day of the sale.

These examples represent only a handful of many ways in which society can acknowledge and respond to the needs of its mothers. If the actual help created for mothers seems small, the psychological impact of these actions is much larger: they make mothers feel welcome and accepted. Mothers find it refreshing to do business where someone takes the time to acknowledge that they may show up with children; that in fact they might even be *expected* to show up with children, and that those children have a respected place in the world.

Opportunities abound for businesses, governments, and other public institutions to help encourage and support all mothers. Judging from suggestions we hear from mothers across the United States and from our own personal experience, there are at least three general areas in which we could all use a helping hand:

**1. Mothers appreciate facilities that make it less difficult to handle children — both physically and psychologically.**

The simplest of chores can become stressful when children must come along to a place that isn't meant for children. For example, standing in a long line at the post office means mothers must keep active, curious children quiet, with nothing to look at and nothing to do, for an undefined and unpredictable amount of time in the company of complete strangers. In addition, because the strangers also have nothing to look at and nothing to do, they often end up watching the children, staring either approvingly or disapprovingly. The pressure this attention puts on a mother is sometimes overwhelming, especially when children are tired or hungry or when it is the last of many other errands and the children are unlikely to be at their best behavior. Though a mother can rarely anticipate such circumstances, she often feels she is somehow responsible when they occur. In such instances, the smallest gesture can be a relief: a table in the corner with a few children's books, a display meant to catch the eye of children, a box of crayons and some scrap paper for children to draw on (and perhaps a bulletin board displaying the artwork of past small "customers").

Obviously, most businesses do not consciously discourage the patronage of a mother with young children. But they unconsciously turn away a mother's business when they do not acknowledge or respond to her needs.

**2. Mothers want to meet other mothers.**

There was a time when it took several generations of people to raise a child — when grandparents and aunts and cousins took as much interest in a child's well-being as his parents did. However, it is rare for a mother today to have her extended family nearby or for them even to be available if she does.

Mothers at home, who often lack an "automatic" social network like those at most workplaces, have a special need to establish close friendships. Writes Genevieve Staiano, from Rego Park, New York: "I am a new mother who feels a need to nurture my son during what I consider to be a very crucial time in his development. It is a financial burden as my husband must work two jobs to support us. It is an emotional burden as well, for most everyone I know — new parent or not — works. I feel definite isolation, and as this was never my 'style,' I find it a most difficult adjustment. Any unique information as to new ideas for making new friends in similar circumstances would be most greatly appreciated."

Teresa Sawyer of Greensboro, North Carolina, says, "I've been home with my son for one year. Homemaking is a challenging career. My friends from high school and college are out climbing career ladders and asking me why on earth a person with my abilities isn't doing the same. Since I began staying home, I've come to realize how important it is to be around other mothers at home. We need encouragement and support from each other because our profession often does not receive such from society." A mother from Cleveland, Ohio, comments, "I need support on a personal level. Even though I belong to a local church body, I find I am in a minority when it comes to staying home and raising my children. I feel like I need help from others like myself."

### 3. Mothers need help getting relief from a continuous job.

Another result of the dispersion of the extended family is that mothers, particularly mothers at home, rarely have a break from their work. Secretaries take coffee breaks; lawyers take lunch breaks; and doctors go on vacation. But mothers are on the job twenty-four hours a day, every day of the year. While many resourceful mothers exchange babysitting hours with friends, establish neighborhood babysitting co-ops, and take advantage of Mothers Day Out programs, more innovative services are critically needed. Experimental programs, ranging from foster grandparenting to high school students who receive child development credit for assisting local mothers, already exist throughout the country. Hopefully, these and other new initiatives will continue to develop and expand.

# Women Who Want To Be Home With Children Need Our Help

In addition to these general areas of need, society should exert special effort to help one important but overlooked group of mothers — those who want to stay home with their children, but find themselves in circumstances that prevent them from doing so.

In April 1984, we expressed the following at a congressional hearing before the U.S. House of Representatives Select Committee on Children, Youth, and Families:

> At this time, most efforts to solve the nation's child care problems center around discovering ways to create more day-care and ways to up-grade the quality of that care. Based on the information coming to us in the form of letters and phone calls from mothers of all backgrounds and circumstances, we strongly suggest that another approach to the problem be investigated — that of bringing home the many mothers who do work, who would rather not be in the paid labor force, who would rather not have their children in day-care in the first place. These mothers, who work only because of economic and social pressures, could be given incentives to remain home with their children. Taking their children out of day-care would make more care available to the mothers who still choose to work.

> Mothers who do require day-care for their children clearly must have access to the best care available. But they are not going to get it from an over-burdened child care system. Seldom do "more" and "quality" go hand-in-hand, and in the case of an issue so deeply human as child care, this is particularly so. We cannot legislate or exercise quality controls over the capacity of one human being to love and care for another. If the child care experiences we hear about from many former and current working mothers is an accurate indication of the kind of child care most mothers are finding, then perhaps the attempt to create more day-care merely hits the symptom rather than the root of the problem.

> Our mail indicates that many mothers are working simply to provide economic stability for their families, and that they view child care as a necessary evil rather than as an acceptable alternative. A mother from Fairfax, Virginia, writes, "You are quite right when you state there is little else besides money drawing mothers to salaried jobs. I work with large numbers of such women both in my 9-5 job and in my volunteer work as director of a women's center."

More subtle than economic pressures to work, but possibly more of an influence on the state of child care in the nation, is the social pressure mothers feel. In the past twenty years, we have fostered a generation of young people who have heard nothing but put-downs about child-rearing. They have been massively encouraged to "do something more important" with their lives. Mothering has no prestige. While we as a nation continue to respect motherhood, we have little respect for its mothers..... When it becomes increasingly evident that the business of raising children is beneath the national dignity, then intelligent, skilled, compassionate people are not likely to want the job. Nor are they likely to want to staff day-care centers to take care of other people's children.

...[T]housands of mothers working both inside and outside the home want desperately to raise their own children. If you help them find a way to do that, both working mothers and mothers at home will benefit... As it stands now, economically and socially, many mothers feel pressured to work. Economic and social incentives for mothers who want to be at home would at last present women with a fair balance of opportunity — the first genuine "choice" they've had in a long time.

In 1988, our publication, WELCOME HOME, surveyed readers on the topic of child care. The response was overwhelming. We found that today's mothers are immensely concerned about the feasibility of caring for their children at home. Suggestions on how to make that choice an easier one poured into our office. In fact, our continued correspondence from mothers across the nation strongly indicates that the establishment of economic incentives and social support for those who prefer to raise their own children at home would have a positive impact on many families, perhaps most families.

Here are some of the ideas mothers told us would make a difference:

## 1. PROVIDE TAX RELIEF FOR FAMILIES WITH CHILDREN

Though most public discussion about how to help families laments the financial challenges of rearing children, the economic forces which have made it so difficult to live on one income are rarely examined in detail. There is, however, increasing bi-partisan agreement that increased taxation and inflation have too long eroded family income. Of all the suggestions received by our organization, tax relief is mentioned most often by far. Specifics include:

### A. Reduce the tax burden on families in general.

A mother of three from Butler, Pennsylvania, writes: "Parents should not be taxed to a degree that they cannot provide for children. The government should stop spending and lower taxes."

### B. Increase the amount of the personal exemption.

Writes a mother from Rexburg, Idaho: "Increasing the dependent exemption gives every family a financial boost. Then the mother can afford to choose to stay home and raise her own children or a family can afford to pay for day-care of their choice."

In fact, the personal exemption of the federal tax code was designed to protect most of a median family income from taxation. In 1948, a family of four at the median income paid 0.3% of its income in federal taxes compared to 9.1% today. In 1992, the personal exemption, at $2150, would have to have been nearly $8000 to restore its value to that of the 1948 exemption.

### C. Institute an additional tax credit or deduction for each preschool child, regardless of the parents' work status.

Such a policy would give parents additional income which they could then apply toward the kind of child care they prefer — whether parental or some kind of substitute care.

### D. Make the Dependent Care Tax Credit equitable.

Currently, this tax credit reimburses parents for documented substitute child care expenses up to $2000 per child regardless of family income. Those families whose relatives help provide child care, those who work at home, or those who have "tag-team" arrangements (mother and father share the care as they split work shifts) are not able to claim this credit because they usually do not pay for child care.

One suggestion for improving it is to limit those who receive the credit to families with low incomes. Another recommendation which is gaining support is to expand the eligibility for this credit. Whether or not the parents work or one parent stays home, all families would receive a tax credit for each dependent child.

## 2. ENCOURAGE FAMILY-FRIENDLY EMPLOYMENT PRACTICES

The workplace is finally acknowledging the need for employees to feel harmony between work and home, and many exciting changes

---

Opportunities for an Enterprising America

are taking place. However, not all "family-friendly" policies or services necessarily support a specific family's needs or time together.

For example, day-care for sick children should not replace the option to take time off with a sick child. Nor should the availability of on-site child care be used to pressure employees to work overtime or to return to their jobs sooner than they desire after the birth of a child.

As family-friendly work options become more available, mothers and fathers will have to evaluate which changes will truly meet the needs of their families. The following are suggestions most often made to us:

**A. Increase the availability of part-time positions.**

According to *U.S. News and World Report* (June 20, 1988), in a 1988 survey of the child care needs of Du Pont Corporation employees, 33% of fathers said they were interested in part-time work to accommodate children, compared to 18% who had been interested in part-time work in 1985. Meanwhile, 55% of the women surveyed were interested in part-time work both survey years.

Traditionally, part-time work has involved hourly wage jobs with few or no benefits. Furthermore, managerial, professional, or highly technical positions were rarely part-time. Today, this situation is changing dramatically, as greater numbers of well-educated women and men have sought opportunities such as shortened work weeks and combination work-at-home options.

From Vallejo, California, a mother of one preschooler writes: "My only complaint is that usually twice a year my boss pesters me a lot to work more hours. He doesn't see the value of having a happy, part-time worker compared to an unhappy full-time employee. [We need] availability of flexible part-time work at a reasonable wage (i.e. being well-compensated for expert work even though it is part-time)." A part-time librarian and mother of two from Fredericksburg, Virginia, reports: "[We need] availability of part-time work with decent benefits! Often part-time jobs have minimal benefits and this is discriminatory."

**B. Increase the availability of flex-time (or flexible schedule) jobs.**

These positions allow employees to vary their starting and quitting times, while still working a full-time workweek. Parents often desire this option in order to be available to their children before and after traditional school hours.

## C. Encourage more job-sharing situations.

Job-sharing is a form of part-time work in which two employees share the responsibilities of one full-time position. Usually, salaries and benefits are prorated by the number of hours each person works. Many mothers seek job-sharing arrangements in order to maintain their careers and yet spend more time at home than a full-time position would permit.

## D. Allow children to accompany parents "on the job" when reasonable.

Many parents find that they prefer to have their children with them while they work in situations as varied as retail establishments, medical practices, nursery schools, farms, etc. Recognizing that there may be reasonable limits to the presence of children in some workplaces, the potential for including children in their parents' work lives should be further explored.

## E. Provide leave for the care of sick family members.

An issue of great concern to all parents is the ability to take off work to care for a sick child or to care for preschool children when a stay-at-home spouse is sick. A part-time social worker and mother of two from Maryland suggests a "compensatory time" arrangement for salaried employees where overtime hours "can be counted later as regular work hours for things like staying home with sick children." Such flexibility is also critical for employees who need to care for sick or elderly relatives.

## F. Establish creative options for mothers on maternity leave.

Although many employers are now recognizing the benefits of good parental leave policies, alternatives are needed for mothers who would prefer to leave work for over a year or for an indefinite period of time. Ideally, mothers who want to care for their children full-time would be able to choose an open-ended arrangement that allows a continuing relationship with their place of employment. For example, employers could maintain "open" personnel files on such employees. They also could keep them informed about organizational changes and events; give them opportunities to update their knowledge and skills; and could offer them occasional temporary assignments or other flexible work options. While companies would not be expected to guarantee a mother the same job she left when she returns to her workplace, they would provide her with an equivalent opportunity based on her prior experience.

A mother from Arlington, Virginia, explains, "I see myself as on an extended leave from the paid work force. I fully expect that the education and skills I acquired before I had children as well as those I've gained as a mother at home will be valuable to a future employer."

## 3. ESTABLISH BETTER OPPORTUNITIES FOR HOME-BASED WORK

Home-based businesses and employment opportunities have been growing for years. Thousands of letters received by Mothers At Home not only support this trend but indicate that many more mothers *and* fathers would work from home if they knew how to begin or could find cultural and practical support for their desire. Some ideas for supporting home-based employment:

**A. Repeal prohibitions and cut the "red tape" for home-based employment.**

Outdated and arbitrary laws at every level of government currently prohibit or make difficult various kinds of home-based employment, including even simple at-home work that would not disrupt residential living. It's time to review the impact of tax policies, zoning and commercial regulations, local licensing practices, and other laws that affect home businesses.

**B. Help employers explore the many ways in which they can use home workers.**

The possibilities for employees to work efficiently from home are expanding with advances in technology, as are the kinds of services a home business can provide to larger corporations. Writes a mother from Gloucester, New Jersey: "I do not want to go back to work because I feel there is no one that could give my baby the love I can give him. Even though I want to raise my child at home, my husband and I cannot afford it unless I find work I can do in my own home. I am an electronic assembler and have seven years of experience. I heard some companies let you do work at home, but I do not know where to find the information."

**C. Encourage banks to examine ways to help home businesses — with loans, advice, and other services.**

Explains a single mother from Baltimore, Maryland: "I receive no child support, but I was determined to stay with my daughter. With the help of my father-in-law, I got a lease on a word processor, and for almost three years I have been working from my home and taking care of my daughter. But the business will not survive unless I can expand, and I can't get any credit or find an investor. I don't want to leave home."

**D. Create job banks and other community resources for individuals interested in earning an income at home.**

Job banks already exist in many communities which could easily expand to include information about home-based employment opportunities. Distribution of information about how to maintain job skills or develop new ones while at home, how to start a home business, or how to find a company that employs home workers would also be helpful. These services would not only benefit parents seeking home employment opportunities but many other individuals as well, such as those whose physical handicaps and financial situations limit their mobility and employment choices. A mother from Bryan, Ohio, writes: "I work as a bank secretary, and am very grateful to have a job in such a good environment. I work out of economic necessity, however, and have always longed to be at home. Do you perhaps have a pamphlet suggesting ways a family can get along on one income and/or how I could stay at home and still earn money?"

**E. Work to make health insurance available and affordable to those who are self-employed.**

Many letters have indicated that the primary reason a mother is employed full-time when she would rather have part-time employment is to qualify for health insurance. This becomes necessary because her husband either receives no such coverage or is self-employed and cannot afford the premiums.

**F. Encourage the formation of home business cooperatives or networks.**

Home businesses could be given opportunities to join together to purchase supplies, hire consultants, use administrative and computer services, participate in group insurance and other benefit plans, share marketing and advertising expenses, and enjoy other advantages that are often too expensive for a single home business owner.

# 4. IMPROVE HOMEMAKER SECURITY AND OPPORTUNITY

While many mothers express a deep personal commitment or yearning to care for their own children at home, they also describe frustration at pervasive cultural disregard for their work as well as government and corporate policies which do not support homemakers. Some of their suggestions include:

**A. Encourage businesses to recognize skills that are developed outside of paid employment.**

The maturity of a person who has had the daily responsibility of caring for children should be viewed as an employment asset. A means of crediting parents for skills developed while nurturing children, managing a home, and giving volunteer service in the community would help potential employers recognize and evaluate unpaid but worthwhile experience.

**B. Increase the amount of tax-deductible money a homemaker can contribute to an IRA.**

Comments a mother from Illinois: "I am appalled that since I have no personal income I cannot contribute more than $250 to my IRA. Legislation should be drafted and passed immediately by Congress so that I can make a full $2000/IRA contribution each year. Does the government think my retirement will be any cheaper than my husband's? And statistically I may outlive him!!!" Other forms of homemaker pension plans should also be explored.

**C. Make college education and job training more available and affordable to mothers.**

The current student college loan program could include qualified homemakers seeking further education.

Furthermore, at-home mothers could benefit from college classes and other training programs that are increasingly accessible through the expanded use of computers and video.

## 5. STRENGTHEN FAMILY ECONOMIC SECURITY

As a nation, we need to investigate the economic forces that are combining to make it nearly impossible to raise a family on one income. Many women who write to us are afraid that they will not be able to meet the financial challenges inherent in rearing a child from birth through a college education. Not only do we hear from mothers in the work force who want desperately to come home; we hear from just as many mothers now at home who express genuine fear that they will be forced back into the labor force before they would choose it. Three areas that receive frequent mention are:

**A. Affordable housing must become more readily available to young families.**

According to University of Maryland economist Frank Levy, payments for a typical house in the 1950's represented about 14% of an average thirty-year-old's gross income. Today, a median-priced house would claim 44% of that income. Writes one mother: "Financially we can manage pretty well, yet we may never have a single family home (the American dream). [We] have made compromises in our dreams so that I can be with my children while they are young." Many parents indicate that paying a mortgage or even paying rent on an adequate home is their families' biggest financial worry, and the factor that may push many mothers into the paid labor force before their families are ready.

**B. Insurance options should be created that recognize the needs of young families, including the special needs of families with one parent at home.**

A mother of two from the Washington, D.C. area states, "I believe that my family is vulnerable because although I have purchased life insurance, my insurance agent tells me that I cannot get disability insurance since it is based on a percentage of one's earnings. Yet, if I were to become disabled, who would care for my children? We could not afford to pay someone else to do my job. The insurance agent has no answer for me."

**C. Tax-free savings plans (similar to IRAs) could be instituted to help young families save in advance for the expenses of rearing children and purchasing homes.**

Explains the Virginia mother of two who suggested this idea: "They would be able to draw on it after birth or adoption of a child, either to offset the cost of a lost income of a stay-at-home parent or to pay for other child care. It could also be used toward the purchase of a first home."

## 6. HELP CREATE COMMUNITIES THAT BETTER SUPPORT FAMILIES

Families today rarely have the benefit of close physical proximity to their extended family. Also, most communities lack the kinds of events or enterprises that link people to a sense of purpose. It is often difficult for adults to develop strong mentor relationships with others to support them in the challenges of rearing children. Community-building activities and local accommodations for families with children should serve to support parents. Some suggestions follow:

**A. Encourage businesses and other public places to make parents and children feel welcome.**

Although public places are gradually becoming more sensitive to parents with young children, many other changes should be made. At the very least a chalkboard, a small table with chairs and books, or some other simple diversion could be provided in the places where parents struggle to wait with children (such as bank lobbies, doctors' waiting rooms, and post offices). Infant changing facilities should be available in both women's and men's public restrooms. In addition, parents would welcome lounges for nursing mothers and facilities that accomodate strollers.

**B. Develop better resources for parents seeking to improve parenting skills and other skills related to family life.**

Almost all parents feel the need for some kind of tutoring or advice from those who have already weathered the storms of parenthood. Whether in the form of library-like information centers, workshops and seminars, or simple forums for exchanging ideas with peers, parents need a place to go with their parenting questions and concerns.

**C. Help prepare the younger generation to successfully handle family responsibilities.**

There is already a push in the educational system to teach teenagers the basics of child development, family finance, and other practical skills for daily living. However, nothing can replace the opportunity to interact directly with children and to hear about real life decisions and experiences from adults within their community. Many mothers tell us that no one ever tried to explain to them the emotional impact of parenthood; therefore, they made financial and career commitments before bearing children without regard to what they and their children might truly need later.

◆　　◆　　◆

Changes like those suggested above are becoming reality through the efforts of many people. Across the nation, mothers are taking actions such as these:

• Protesting whenever they see or hear a misrepresentation of the "working" mother statistics.

---

• Monitoring the media by responding to inaccuracies and biases in stories about mothers' lives.

• Writing to local, state, and national political leaders about issues concerning mothers.

• Encouraging parents to develop flexibility in their places of employment so that they can spend more time nurturing their families.

• Reminding others that our work ethic should include respect for the work of caring for one's own children.

• Working to create communities that support families.

How a mother feels about society depends on so many factors that it is impossible to speak for everyone. There are, however, some feelings which almost all mothers share. Mothers today do not relate to the media stereotypes of either the working mother or the mother at home, and all mothers will feel relief as these caricatures slowly disappear. Most mothers today are anxious to feel respect for the choices they have made for themselves and their children, and would like an end to the uncomfortable prodding to take sides in a media-fed "war."

More importantly, mothers want changes in their lives that would result from a society better attuned to their needs. Their ideas for such improvements reflect the insight of those who live the problem and are willing to work for the solution. Joining together in bringing those changes to pass is crucial to the well-being of our children and to our entire society.

# The Coming Revolution in American Motherhood

**M**otherhood is indeed in the midst of a radical transformation. There are real and permanent changes taking place. But these changes are *not* those that are presumed and frequently discussed by the media.

After a decade of deep internal conflict, a new American mother is emerging — one who will soon comprise an unquestioned majority. She is the mother who is learning to put family first without putting herself last. She is the mother who is willing to creatively experiment with her options until she finds a balance between personal and economic needs and her desire to spend more time at home. She is the mother who is shifting her work hours, dropping to part-time employment, starting a home business, or quitting work completely — whatever it takes to give priority to her home and to those she loves.

We who are rearing children today have been told that combining motherhood and full-time employment is the wave of the future. But we are not convinced. After seeking fulfillment in the workplace, too many of us are feeling much like the miller's daughter in the fairy tale "Rumpelstiltskin." Giving up our children in order to live up to the promise that we could spin straw into gold sounded fine before our sons and daughters were born. But once children have come into our lives — to enrich us and entreat us and reveal to us new depths and dimensions — we cannot bear to give away to anyone else the rewards of the mothering years.

We are discovering that motherhood is not an unfulfilling dead end, as many of us have been led to believe. Rather, it presents us with great opportunities to enlarge the spectrum of our own possibilities. And we are learning that many of the frustrations associated with full-time motherhood are not the mark of a meaningless, unrewarding job. Instead, they are the result of engaging in a work that no one else comprehends — of taking on the challenge of our lives without the benefit of a supportive society to share either our vision or our burdens, our victories or our defeats.

America's mothers are discarding theories about self-fulfillment and the rearing of children in favor of personal experience. And experience has taught them that nourishing family relationships and strengthening the spirit of "home" are endeavors that require considerable effort, unrestrained energy, and a surprising amount of time. After investigating the shortcuts promoted by an outspoken few, today's mothers are beginning to want to spend that energy and effort, and most of all, that time.

Women who are choosing home today are not part of a dying breed coming back into vogue. They are not fanatics, simplistically hanging onto the apron strings of tradition. They are the flesh and blood product of a bold and aggressive women's movement — the very women who have been taught to stand up for what they believe, whether or not it is popular and whether or not it is accepted. And they are doing just that.

# Why Mothers of Young Children Don't Write a Lot of Books

**I**'ll bet a lot of people who read this book think that authors just sit down and write a manuscript — write and write and write until the whole thing looks pretty good, at which point they give it to a publisher who puts a cover on it and sends it along to bookstores all over the country.

That's what *we* thought, too, when we signed up for this project.

Although we suspected that one mother alone might have a hard time writing a whole book, we thought that the three of us working hard on a subject in which we have been immersed for three years would surely produce a decent manuscript in six weeks. Allowing for the surprises that always enliven a mother's life, we wisely added another four weeks to the deadline when we signed the contract.

We underestimated by nearly three months. Even committees of mothers, we found out, don't have time to write books.

The first "official" day of the project, I woke early (after spending most of the night up with my two-year-old) to help my third-grade daughter type a report about Robert Frost. A few minutes before the school bus was due, my fourth-grade son became frantic over a misplaced permission slip. We searched the house, but never found it; meanwhile, my daughter — whose report sat unfinished on my desk — missed the bus.

We finished the typing and I drove her to school, dropping the two-year-old at a friend's house to play on my way back, so I could have time to write while the baby napped. But the baby refused to nap. No matter. After spending the morning trying to walk her to sleep, I had just laid her in the crib when the school clinic called and informed me that my son was sick to his stomach. Back up to the school I went — after waking the baby and retrieving the two-year-old.

With teenaged sitters still in school and most adult sitters unwilling to commit to a "six weeks only" job, finding time to write became an adventure. Television was my first (and in the end, best) resource. (This in a house where the rule had always been: Television on Friday nights only!) It was, however, a poor substitute mother. Once I tried diverting my two-year-old with "Sesame Street," but she cried at the sight of the "monsters" and opted for a documentary on gorillas instead! The baby was playing quietly in a corner, so I stole away for a relatively long period of time, working on the book until an unusually shiny baby came crawling into the bedroom, covered with Vaseline from head to toe. The two-year-old make-up artist followed, obviously disturbed that her client had fled. So much for that writing session!

And subsequent sessions were little better. I did most of my writing in the midst of squirt gun fights, requests for gum, piles of unsorted laundry, spilled juice, an unexpected visit by old friends, stacks of unopened mail, a short stay by little cousins while their mother was hospitalized, art lessons, soccer practice, phone calls from Bob the Computer, and nearly everything else. The worst, I think, was when the bedroom door jammed and I was locked inside until my husband climbed in a window and removed the hinges while my sister threw her weight against the door to knock it down — leaving my "office" doorless in a small rambler with six lively children. Or perhaps the worst was when my husband was sent out of town to Austin, Texas, three days before science fair projects were due. (The same thing happened last year, except he was sent to Austin, Nevada. Now, I don't want to sound superstitious, but I have checked the atlas and there are five more "Austins" to go in the United States alone.)

So you see, there is a good reason why books about mothering at home don't fill the shelves of local bookstores. The would-be authors are simply too busy practicing motherhood to spend their time preaching about it.

**—Cheri Loveless**

---

It was Memorial Day — my husband had the day off from work and the kids were home from school. Since my first activity of the day was to give my husband a badly needed haircut, I asked him to read through a chapter of the book and comment on it while I cut his hair.

I started cutting and he started reading. Soon, a child appeared saying, "Daddy, you promised you'd make pancakes for breakfast this morning." After providing reassurance that the pancakes would be started as soon as the haircut was finished, he went back to reading. Another child came in saying, "Daddy, can't you build us a swing set today? You're home today. Can't you do it?" This was a little harder to deal with than the pancakes, but after discussing it, he went back to his reading. Then:

"Daddy, when will Mommy be done with your haircut?"

"Daddy, I'm hungry. Why haven't you made the pancakes yet?"

"Daddy, will you take us on a bike ride today?"

"Daddy, couldn't you please build the swing set?"

After about ten minutes of this, my husband put down the chapter and said, "It's crazy for mothers to write books. I can't even read *one* chapter! How do you expect to write a *whole book???*"

**—Janet Dittmer**

---

I sit here with my daughters at my feet, writing a book. Wisps of curly blond hair tumble over a Superman T-shirt, bare legs folded into a triangle base that not only holds the little body upright but also serves as a stage for the dolls and all their trappings. Tiny fingers try again and again to fasten a doll dress. Finally, matter-of-factly, without a hint of frustration or embarrassment, the request comes: "Mommy, will you put this dress on Rose Petal for me?" I do. She smiles and goes back to her make-believe world.

Surely, I have the best of all worlds.

Another little head, this time a fuzzy one, appears at the side of my chair. Watching me type only holds her interest for the shortest moment. "Ahdaaa!" she shouts in greeting. I acknowledge the salutation. Still this is not enough. "AHDAAAAAAAA!" she tries a little louder, adding a slight fuss at the end of the phrase. "I know. You want up on my lap. Just a minute, silly, I'm trying to finish a paragraph."

She turns and crawls off, and I think I have won. But, as usual, I have merely been outsmarted. She scoots purposefully over to my box of files for the book. Pulling herself up against the side of the box, she reaches long over the edge and grabs the first folder. Out comes the contract with the publisher. Out comes the preliminary outline. Out comes . . .

Oh, well. Better save the rest. She gets her way and I gently lift her onto my knees. She lunges at the computer keyboard and types a line of "vvvvvvv's" across the page. A few more interpolations and I decide to try a diversionary tactic.

"Look at this great basket of toys!" I exclaim, transporting her across the room and plopping her in front of a colorful array of baby knickknacks, some from as far back as 1975. This time she takes the bait and I return to my writing.

Surely, this is the best of all worlds.

—**Cheri Loveless**

---

I had the day all planned. After going to an 8:30 a.m. meeting at the school with one of my boys' teachers, I would spend the whole morning working on the book while my little girl attended preschool.

My first clue that the day might not go so smoothly was when all of us (my husband included) overslept. We woke up exactly thirty minutes before we were supposed to walk out the door for the appointment at school. Six people raced around throwing clothes on, gobbling down breakfast, bumping into each other, furiously packing lunches, and trying to find everything everyone needed for the day.

After the appointment, which we somehow managed to get to only three minutes late, I remembered that I would have to make a trip to the *Welcome Home* office that morning. I needed to pick up brochures and sample newsletters to take to a mothers' group where I would be speaking the following morning. Normally, I could go to the office any time of day or night, but the lock on the door had just been replaced and I didn't have the new key. Some of my book-writing time would just have to be spent running this errand during the 8:00-12:00 office hours.

Before going to the preschool, I stopped off at home to pick up some personal letters and bills that needed to be mailed. I also picked up a few *Welcome Home* papers since I would be going to the office, as well as an envelope containing several dollars in cash for some sample newsletters I had sold. Then I put my daughter in the car, stopped at my mailbox to leave my personal mail for the postal carrier, and drove to the preschool. After getting my daughter settled there, I drove on to the office and hurried in to pick up the brochures and newsletters. I collected what I needed, distributed the papers I had brought in, and handed our office manager the envelope containing the cash. I began explaining where the money had come from, but she looked strangely at the envelope. What I had handed her was not the envelope of cash, but a stamped letter to my insurance company that should have been sitting in my mailbox at home. That meant, of course, that sitting in my mailbox instead was the envelope of cash.

I drove home as fast as I dared, but the mailbox flag was down and the envelope of money had been picked up with the other letters. I had only penciled "WH $" on the front of the envelope, so I knew no one would figure out who it belonged to. I called the post office, explained my sad story, and answered all kinds of questions. After the interrogation, the postal worker promised to look through our mail carrier's bags as soon as they came in.

By now, my plan for a quiet morning at home working on the book had turned into a ridiculous escapade. There was only a little time left before I needed to pick up my daughter, and I was so agitated, I couldn't concentrate anyway. So much for well-laid plans.

P.S. I didn't get anything done on the book that morning, but I *did* get the money back. The post office called in the afternoon to say they had found the "WH $" envelope which they returned to my mailbox the following day.

—**Janet Dittmer**

Much of my writing for this book was done at red lights, in the pediatrician's waiting room, and standing in the checkout line at the grocery store. My purse is filled with "book" notes which were written on old receipts; complete paragraphs, and sometimes even whole pages, were squeezed into the available space on an outdated shopping list. I have tried to grab the time to write, like a child reaches out to claim the brass ring on a merry-go-round — both of us, most of the time, missing our mark.

Thoughts about the topics I have addressed in this book almost never showed up for scheduled appointments at the typewriter. Instead, they waltzed in when I was trying to negotiate bumper-to-bumper traffic, or when I was absorbed in deep discussion with a good friend on an entirely different topic. Somehow the time and/or excuses had to be found, given the resources at hand (in my most desperate hour, I wrote on a napkin, with a lipstick), to commit additional thoughts to paper. When the thoughts stopped coming, I would simply fish out all the little stubs, lists, napkins, and receipts from my purse, type them out legibly on a sheet or two of paper, and proceed from there.

Days, and even weeks, passed simply trying to clear my head of it all, so I could begin again. On those days, I stared at my blank computer screen until I was sure I could see a heart monitor: blip . . . blip . . . blip . . . Buzzzzzzzzzzzzz, like on an old "Marcus Welby, M.D." re-run when suddenly there was nothing left but a dull hum and a simple wavy line to indicate where life once was.

Usually, Cheri or Janet would call and spark a new thought or help develop a fledgling idea, and we would be off to the races again. In fact, we often held two- and three-hour meetings via telephone and wrote with each other via computer modem in order to tend to the needs of our assorted children and their diverse schedules.

Through it all, helping to write this book has been an enormous joy to me. Where tensions, disagreements, and needy egos could easily have been the order of the day, the three of us have honestly spent most of the time locked in fascinated, lively discussion, punctuated by spontaneous laughter.

I have loved our work together. I will miss it very much.

—**Linda Burton**

Tomorrow is it: the deadline.

Months of stealing a few minutes here and there in front of the computer — mostly in the middle of the night — will be over. Months of watching the pages of the manuscript "pile" grow more slowly than the laundry pile. Months of putting aside little things that really needed my attention. Months of turning aside little people who really wanted my attention. Months of errands run and chores done by a less-than-perfectionist but very proud group of one dad, one baby, and five kids. ("Look, Mom! We scrubbed the floors!" The wood floors, that is.) Months of living the paradox of loving what I was doing but wishing all I were doing was having a slow, easy, hang-around-together summer with my kids.

Tomorrow is the deadline.

I think I'll celebrate by taking everyone out to dinner on my advance money and maybe treating them to a movie after that. Or maybe I'll just spend the day getting to those one hundred house-cleaning things that husbands and children don't seem to notice that have been tapping me on the shoulder since last March. Or perhaps I'll snuggle up on the couch and read an entire book that *someone else* wrote.

So tomorrow is the deadline!

Actually, I think I'll finally try to get some sleep.

**—Cheri Loveless**

# About the Authors

Linda Burton, Janet Dittmer, and Cheri Loveless are the founders of **Mothers At Home** and its publication *Welcome Home*. Through their organization and its network of volunteers, they have provided support for mothers who choose to stay home to nurture their families by publishing educational materials, testifying before Congressional committees, participating in parenting conferences, lecturing, and generally speaking out about motherhood.

Linda Burton, a native of Northern Virginia, attended the College of William and Mary, and spent ten years studying voice, performing in local theatre, and writing — including her own column in a chain of papers in New Jersey. After a career in development and public relations writing, she married and started her family of two sons and one daughter. She currently writes, teaches, and volunteers while raising her children at home.

Janet Dittmer was born and raised in Michigan, where she received a B.S. degree from Michigan State University. After earning an M.A. degree from Oregon State University and working for Stanford Research Institute, she married and began her family, which now numbers six sons and one daughter. In addition to pursuing a variety of hobbies, she gives talks and workshops on time management and home organization.

Cheri Loveless grew up in the suburbs of Washington, D.C. She studied French and history at Brigham Young University before starting her family of five daughters and two sons. While rearing her children at home, she has organized a large food cooperative and co-authored one previous book (*Cut Your Grocery Bills in Half*, Acropolis, 1983). She is actively involved in her children's education, and continues to write and edit for a variety of publishing projects.

# About Mothers At Home™

In 1984, Linda Burton, Janet Dittmer, and Cheri Loveless founded **Mothers At Home**, a non-profit organization devoted to the support of mothers who choose (or would like to choose) to be at home to nurture their families.

This new organization grew quickly. Its goals are: to help mothers at home realize they have made a great choice; to help mothers excel at a job for which no one feels fully prepared; and to correct society's many misconceptions about mothering.

Many volunteers and a small paid staff have carried on the work begun by Linda, Janet and Cheri.

## Welcome Home®

**Mothers At Home** publishes *Welcome Home*, a monthly journal that supports at-home mothers by helping them to speak with each other. Readers participate directly by contributing articles and art work, thus reflecting the varied talents and unique perspectives of many different women at home.

## Speaking Out For Mothers

After receiving thousands of letters and speaking to dozens of audiences, the **Mothers At Home** founders were surprised and inspired by what they had learned about mothers. In 1986, Linda, Janet, and Cheri first wrote *What's a Smart Woman Like You Doing At Home*. Since that time, **Mothers At Home** volunteers have continued to research, write, and speak out about the needs of families. The staff communicates with mothers' groups, the media, public policy organizations, government officials, and others, providing public policy information and analyses through *Welcome Home*.

## More Resources

The staff of **Mothers At Home** continues to identify mothers' special interests and needs. They realized that new mothers, faced with significant physical, emotional, and social changes, are especially in need of assistance while they make the transition into motherhood.

In response the staff created *Discovering Motherhood*, a book especially for women in the early years of motherhood. It shares the thoughts and feelings of many mothers through essays, informative articles, humor, poetry, resource ideas, and more — to convey the essence of a home-centered life.

## A Family-Friendly Organization

The **Mothers At Home** volunteers and staff have work options which include part-time and job-share positions, flexible schedules, and home-based work. The organization is housed in a family-friendly office located in northern Virginia, outside of Washington, D.C. Staff members and volunteers can meet and work together including their children at anytime.

An order form for *What's A Smart Woman Like You Doing At Home?* and other **Mothers At Home** publications is included in this book. Additional inquiries can be directed to:

**Mothers At Home**™
P.O. Box 2192
8310A Old Courthouse Road
Vienna, Virginia  22182

*A one-year subscription brings 12 issues of our 32-page journal.*

# Join the thousands of mothers who communicate every month through the pages of *Welcome Home*®

Since 1984, thousands of mothers across the country have found support and a sense of community through the pages of our monthly journal, **Welcome Home**. Dedicated to supporting mothers who choose to be home to nurture their families, all of its articles, essays, poems, and illustrations are created and donated by mothers. **Welcome Home** reflects the varied talents and perspectives of women at home, offering stories about our struggles and successes, informative articles about family life and public policy issues, humor, poetry, and more.

Since our very first issue, mothers with diverse experiences and personal situations have responded with gratitude and enthusiasm...

*My mothering gets a real boost every month when **WH** arrives. I suffer from periodic doubts about this against-the-mainstream choice I've made, and wonder: do I do a "good enough" job at it to justify it? Hearing other mothers' ideas and insights and sharing their experience and enthusiasm helps to reassure me that, yes, I've made a good choice, and to remind me that it's even a fun one. Thank you — this is worth a lot!* — W.McV., Belle Fontaine, Ohio

*Your articles inspired me and supported me... thank you for coming along just when I needed you the most.* — S.R., Needham, MA

*I am thrilled to renew my subscription — you have the most affirmative magazine on the market for parenting. It is truly a unique combination of information for the mind, heart, soul, and gut!* — A.S., Schoharie, New York

*I enjoy the humor and the seriousness of it all... The feelings, thoughts, and happenings are all so familiar. The ideas are so helpful... the people who contribute are so REAL.* — J.B., Trenton, New Jersey

*From the first issue I was in love — with the concept, simplicity, support, and the wonderful feeling of sisterhood I felt with the other mothers. Each issue is like a spiritual transfusion for my soul. I used to read it as I'd nurse my baby, and now I carry it around with me as I chase him around. I read it in snips and snatches, taking small doses when time allows. I feel renewed and full of greater understanding, appreciation, and love for my family and my very important job.* — S.R., South Bend, Indiana

# ORDER FORM

**Mothers At Home®** • 8310A Old Courthouse Road • Vienna VA 22182

Your Name _____

Street Address _____

City _____ State _____ Zip _____

Phone ( _____ ) _____

## ❏ I would like to purchase:

|  | Units Ordered | Price |
|---|---|---|

**WELCOME HOME** SUBSCRIPTION(S)

$18 (U.S.), $21 (Canada), $28 (overseas) _____ _____

Sample copy of **Welcome Home**: $2.00 _____ _____

**BOOKS:**

**Discovering Motherhood**: $9.95 + s&h _____ _____

**What's a Smart Woman Like You
     Doing At Home?** : $8.95 + s&h _____ _____

Shipping & handling for books:
add $2.50 for 1st book, $.50 for each additional book. **S&H** _____

**Subtotal** _____

**VA Residents: Add 4.5% sales tax** _____
*(not applicable to subscriptions)*

**TOTAL** _____

## ❏ I would like to help Mothers At Home continue its efforts with a tax-deductible contribution:

General donation in the amount of ........................................................ $ _____

Scholarship fund donation in the amount of .................................... $ _____

(to provide **Welcome Home** subscriptions to needy moms)

**TOTAL ENCLOSED** $ _____

Make check payable to **Mothers At Home,** U.S. funds only.

**Call 1-800-783-4666 for VISA or Mastercard orders (M-F, 9-5 EST)**

---

**GIFTS:** *We will send your recipient a card notifying her of a gift subscription or a gift book.*

Send:

❏ **WH** subscription
❏ **DM** Book
❏ **SW** Book

A Gift From: _____

To Be Sent To:
Name _____

Street Address _____

City _____ State _____ Zip _____

To order additional gifts, please provide the above information
on a separate sheet of paper.

# ORDER FORM

**Mothers At Home®** • 8310A Old Courthouse Road • Vienna VA 22182

Your Name _____

Street Address _____

City _____ State _____ Zip _____

Phone ( _____ ) _____

## ❏ I would like to purchase:

|  | Units Ordered | Price |
|---|---|---|

**WELCOME HOME** SUBSCRIPTION(S)

$18 (U.S.), $21 (Canada), $28 (overseas)     ____     _____

Sample copy of **Welcome Home**: $2.00     ____     _____

**BOOKS:**

**Discovering Motherhood**: $9.95 + s&h     ____     _____

**What's a Smart Woman Like You
Doing At Home?** : $8.95 + s&h     ____     _____

Shipping & handling for books:
add $2.50 for 1st book, $.50 for each additional book.     **S&H** _____

**Subtotal** _____

**VA Residents: Add 4.5% sales tax** _____
*(not applicable to subscriptions)*

**TOTAL** _____

## ❏ I would like to help Mothers At Home continue its efforts with a tax-deductible contribution:

General donation in the amount of.......................................... $ _____

Scholarship fund donation in the amount of ..................................... $ _____

(to provide **Welcome Home** subscriptions to needy moms)

**TOTAL ENCLOSED** $ _____

Make check payable to **Mothers At Home**, U.S. funds only.

**Call 1-800-783-4666 for VISA or Mastercard orders (M-F, 9-5 EST)**

**GIFTS:** *We will send your recipient a card notifying her of a gift subscription or a gift book.*

Send:

❏ **WH subscription**
❏ **DM Book**
❏ **SW Book**

A Gift From: _____

To Be Sent To:

Name _____

Street Address _____

City _____ State _____ Zip _____

To order additional gifts, please provide the above information
on a separate sheet of paper.